PERFECT PLANTS

GRAHAM RICE

FOREWORD BY ADRIENNE WILD

ANAYA PUBLISHERS LTD
London

First published in Great Britain in 1990 by Anaya Publishers Ltd,
49 Neal Street, London WC2H 9PJ

Text copyright © 1990 Graham Rice

British Library Cataloguing in Publication Data
A CIP record for this book is available from the British Library

ISBN 1-85470-040-5
(Hardback)

ISBN 1-85470-056-1
(Paperback)

Designed by Claudine Meissner

Typeset by Tradespools Ltd, Frome, Somerset

Printed in Great Britain by
Richard Clay Ltd
Bungay, Suffolk
for Anaya Publishers

CONTENTS

Foreword *6* · Introduction *7*

FOREWORD

WELCOME TO *Practical Gardening*'s answer to the problem of choosing just the right plants for your garden. I'm sure you'll find it both interesting and of immense practical use.

This is a book for the plant enthusiast – whether you're new to gardening and find the mass of plants on sale in the garden centre bewildering or have been gardening for some years and know what you like. As long as you love plants you'll find this book helpful, and after all it's the plants that make a garden.

Graham Rice's plant knowledge is reinforced throughout by his practical know-how so that not only can he recommend the pick of garden plants but can also give sound and constructive advice on how to grow them well. There are also plenty of imaginative ideas on where to place the plants in the garden to create the most attractive effect.

All in all, although it's delightful to look at, this is a book to use. I'm sure it will be a trusty companion to novice and expert gardeners alike.

Adrienne Wild

Editor
Practical Gardening

CHOOSING PERFECT PLANTS

THIS IS where I stick my neck out. Choosing the best couple of hundred of all garden plants not only gives me great problems in deciding what to include, but invites the terrible wrath of those who disagree with my selection. And when they realize that their own special favourites have been left out, even gardeners – a notoriously placid race – may begin to turn puce.

But even if your own favourite is missing, you can rest assured that all those I've chosen are splendid and reliable plants. Many of the varieties selected are ones that I have grown myself, the rest I've seen in other gardens. All are guaranteed to bring beauty to your garden provided you give them the little care they deserve.

The range of plants from which gardeners can choose is vast, so this book is written for those who need a little help in choosing from the many thousands of different varieties available in nurseries. But, unless you're a real expert, how do you decide which climber or which small tree to buy? This book does the initial selection for you, presenting information on only the very best plants for flowers, ornamental foliage and fruit, scent as well as a great number of other important characteristics.

I have been very specific in my choice, rather than simply recommending clematis as a good climber or hostas as good foliage plants. In most cases, I've picked out the one or two varieties that are truly exceptional.

But I have imposed some realistic constraints on myself and, as a result, have been reluctant to recommend too many plants that are difficult to find in garden centres and nurseries. But I do break this rule in a chapter on connoisseurs' plants in order to recommend some really choice favourites.

Although, naturally, many of my favourites are included, this is not just a personal selection. I've even included one or two that I do not really like, because I am aware that they are nonetheless superb plants, and very much appreciated by gardeners everywhere.

The only other restriction has been the amount of care and attention the plants need. So those that need winter protection, constant spraying or exceptional growing conditions have been left out of most chapters.

Many thousands of good garden plants that would give anyone pleasure have, of course, been left out in favour of those special few which have that little extra something not always apparent when you see the plants in the garden centre.

Each entry describes the characteristics of the plant and its special features, explains any particular care it needs to thrive and outlines how to propagate it. An important and very useful section gives ideas on how to use each variety in the garden to its best advantage and I have also given a range of alternatives – plants that differ slightly in flower colour perhaps or size. And because no plant is entirely perfect, no matter how wonderful, I have owned up to any problems you really need to know about.

There are over 40,000 different plants available from nurseries. I hope you find this selection helps you to choose those that really will give you the most pleasure for the least trouble.

WHERE PLANTS COME FROM

ALL THE 40,000 varieties that are sold in nurseries and, of course, the 200 specially recommended plants in this book have to come from somewhere – but where?

First of all, some are wild plants that grow naturally in the countryside. These

7

were the first to be taken into cultivation as mankind started to grow plants and they were then simply dug up from the places they grew naturally and moved nearer to habitation. Many were food plants or plants with medicinal properties, but ornamental plants, too, were moved nearer to houses as can still be seen in the wilds of Papua New Guinea where the bush people dig up wild busy Lizzies and replant them around their huts.

More recently this practice of poaching on nature's preserves has led to the dramatic decline of many wild plants, so the lady's slipper orchid, for example, is now reduced to just one single plant in northern England, these orchids having formerly been dug up by the hundred and planted in gardens. Few, if any, of the transplanted orchids survived.

Plants from overseas have also been introduced. The Romans brought many useful plants to the countries they conquered – they also brought their weeds – and, especially since the 17th century, specialist plant collectors have travelled to the remotest corners of the earth, sometimes in great danger, and sought out unknown plants to bring back to the civilized world.

For both scientific and commercial reasons plant collectors were sent out, mainly from Europe, to Asia, America and Australasia and they brought back many thousands of exotic plants which in the 19th century in Europe inspired a fanatical interest in new plants from abroad.

This interest in new and unfamiliar plants is still going on with recent scientific expeditions to Japan, South America and China bringing back seed of previously unknown – or ungrown – plants which after a few years of assessment are finding their way into nurseries.

Unfortunately commercial collecting still goes on and many plants, especially bulbs, are stripped from their natural habitats and imported into Europe and elsewhere for sale to gardeners. Most natural plant populations can withstand the removal of a few specimens occasionally, but collecting on the scale now taking place with millions of wild cyclamen and winter aconites being exported from Turkey every year will eventually lead to the extinction of some species. Fortunately, regulations are now being introduced which control this trade and which will hopefully prevent further damage.

But plants vary, even different plants of the same wild species vary, and this is nature's way of providing ready-made adaptations for survival if conditions change. These variations occur both in the wild and in gardens, and botanists and horticulturalists with a keen eye for such things are able to pick them out and give them individual names.

These chance mutations, or sports as they are sometimes called, crop up all the time and many new plants arise through a keen-eyed gardener spotting a branch on a shrub that looks a little different or, perhaps, a self-sown seedling in the border that seems unusual.

But it wasn't long before gardeners started trying to encourage variation by hybridizing. If you have two plants with different characteristics that you want to bring together in one new plant or if you wish to create an intermediate between the two, pollen can be transferred from one to the other and the plants that grow from the seeds examined carefully. Amongst these seedlings there may be plants that combine the features from the two parents in different ways and those that are useful can be picked out and propagated to form a new variety.

So if you take the pollen from a tall-growing pea plant and use it to fertilize a short-growing pea, you should get some peas of medium height. And if you take the pollen from a red-flowered primrose with red-tinted leaves and use it to fertilize another primrose with yellow flowers and green leaves, you may well get a plant with yellow flowers and red-tinted leaves.

Cyclamens are among the best plants for naturalizing in semi-shade, where they will multiply to form an attractive carpet of ground cover.

Of course nowadays raising new plants has become much more sophisticated and plant breeding is a multinational business, not just in the breeding of agricultural seeds but the breeding of flower seeds too.

But now that the nursery and seed trade has become big business, novelty plants are seen as the key to constant expansion. The problem is that sometimes 'new' plants are introduced which are not actually improvements on existing varieties and may even be old plants with new names. This is one of the tricks I have been aware of in selecting plants for this book.

In the descriptions of the plants I have selected, you will find examples of all the different ways in which plants originate. But it's interesting to note that more than the odd one or two have been developed by ordinary home gardeners with a good eye – it doesn't take a real expert or a multinational company to produce something new and exciting.

PLANT NAMES

ALL PLANTS have Latin names. Many gardeners wonder why this is necessary and complain bitterly that it just makes it more difficult to remember what plants are called. And it's true that bluebell is much easier on the ear and the memory than *Endymion non-scriptus*. But at once we have a demonstration of the problem for it's only in England that the name bluebell refers to this particular plant, the blue-flowered woodland bulb. In Scotland the name is attached to what in England is known as the harebell, *Campanula rotundifolia*. In America the name is attached to at least three quite different plants.

So the use of a standard Latin name enables people all over the world to use the same name for the same plant with no confusion whatsoever.

Botanical names have two parts. The first part, *Campanula* for example, covers a group of plants with broadly similar characteristics. It's like a surname. In many cases this surname refers to some common characteristic of the group. In this case the name is derived from the Latin *campana* meaning a bell and referring to the shape of the flowers. But sometimes the name has no connection with the features of the plants.

The second part of the name is more like a Christian name or forename and pins down one particular plant. Again this name may refer to some special feature of the plant and in this case *rotundifolia* (literally 'round-leaved') refers to the shape of the basal leaves. This second part of the name may also commemorate the person who first found the plant or the area where it grows naturally.

Variants with only slight differences which are found growing naturally are given another Latin name – so a white-flowered form may be called *alba*, and if it is also dwarf form, *minor* may be added.

Variations which occur in gardens and nurseries or are intentionally bred are given vernacular names like 'Orange King', 'Mrs Popple' or 'Sensation' – sometimes these describe the plant, they may commemorate an individual or they may have a less direct connection.

Unfortunately plant names sometimes change. This happens when botanists want to correct the name of a wrongly named plant or when research reveals that a plant has a closer affinity with a group other than that with which it was originally placed. The naming of plants is controlled by internationally agreed rules, which at least ensure a uniformity of approach and which in the long run will greatly reduce the confusion.

Where there are confusions over names amongst the plants I have selected in the book, I have outlined the problem in the entries, indicating the correct name and any alternatives under which the plant may still be sold in garden centres.

TREES

Acer griseum 13
Acer palmatum 'Senkaki' *16*
Betula 'Jermyns' *20*
Betula pendula 'Tristis' *18*
Chamaecyparis lawsoniana 'Lanei' *19*
Cornus kousa var. *chinensis* 16
Laburnum × *watereri* 'Vossii' *15*
Malus 'Golden Hornet' *18*
Prunus 'Cheal's Weeping Cherry' *13*
Prunus serrula 14
Pyrus salicifolia 'Pendula' *15*
Salix caprea 'Pendula' *17*
Sorbus 'Joseph Rock' *12*

YOU HAVE to be careful with trees. It's easy to plant a tree that looks lovely for a few years and then starts to make you uneasy as it grows taller and taller and casts more and more shade. Eventually it becomes so huge that you have to pay an expert to remove it.

So it pays to think before you buy. If you can steel yourself to remove a fifteen-year-old cedar when it's in perfect health and just beginning to look really elegant, then by all means plant one. But why not plant a tree which can be allowed to mature naturally and will still not overshadow your garden and windows at 50?

I've chosen these particular trees either for the long season of interest of their foliage, their attractive bark, their elegant shape, their multi-season interest with perhaps flowers and then fruit, or for their short but spectacular show at one season – though in most small gardens this is something of a luxury. Even in the smallest of gardens there is room for a tree and most gardens will accommodate at least two or three small trees where one large one would be unacceptable.

Five groups of trees predominate, both for their suitability and the range of different types available. The maples, birches, cherries, crab apples and mountain ashes (plus the related whitebeams) between them include many fine small and medium-sized trees, most of which are easy to grow, though the cherries in particular suffer from a very short season of interest.

Finally, a word about propagation. Many of these trees are propagated by grafting. This is a technique in which a twig of the chosen variety is joined to the roots of a stronger-rooting variety to create a more robust specimen. Alternatively, it may be grafted to the top of a stem of a stouter variety to create a weeping standard tree. This is a highly skilled technique and while home gardeners can achieve reasonable results with practice, it's generally more practical to buy plants of varieties requiring this treatment from the nursery or garden centre and concentrate on propagating only those plants which grow from seed, or that root from cuttings or can be divided easily.

Sorbus
'Joseph Rock'

Good all-seasons tree
Deciduous, to 15ft (4.5m)

A DECIDUOUS tree with a narrow crown, this is grown for its flowers, fruits and autumn colour. Growing to about 15ft (4.5m) in ten years, this superb mountain ash makes a neat and narrow crown of branches carrying flat heads of white flowers from mid spring to early summer. These are followed up in late summer with yellow, slightly orange-tinted fruits in generous clusters which hang on the tree well into the autumn. The orangy autumn colour is good too, especially on fertile soils.

Cultivation

Full sun is needed to ensure that plenty of fruit is set and to show it off well. This variety really does need a good soil so is not at its best in gardens such as those on new housing estates. Poor soil can be improved with organic matter before planting but gardens which have been uncultivated for some time may not produce trees that grow well and give the best fruit. Growth will also be slow. Pruning is not usually necessary.

Sorbus 'Joseph Rock' gives good value all year with creamy late spring flowers, good autumn leaf colour and long-lasting fruits.

Propagation

Like many trees, this variety is grafted and this is best left to the experts. Plants raised from the berries are unlikely to produce trees which fruit as well as their parent.

Uses in the garden

It makes a fine feature in a mixed border in a larger garden or as the one specimen tree in a smaller one.

Alternatives

There are many other varieties of mountain ash with good fruits. Rather slower in growth is *Sorbus hupehensis* with pink-tinged, white berries. *S. cashmiriana* is often little more than a large shrub and has pure white berries and rather better autumn colour.

Acer griseum

Paperbark maple
Deciduous, to 12ft (3.6m)

THE PAPERBARK maple grows naturally in China and was introduced to Britain in 1907. It is a charming deciduous tree with a compact head. Growth is slow and in ten years the height is usually about 12ft (3.6m). A 30-ft (9-m) tree is exceptional. The main attraction is the peeling bark which develops on branches over about three years old and especially on the trunk. The mahogany-brown outer bark rolls back to reveal the golden, cinnamon-brown colour underneath. In the autumn the foliage turns an attractive dark orange shade. Its slow growth may be seen as a drawback and it tends to be expensive.

Cultivation

It is happy in most soils but does object to thin soils over chalk or limestone and does not thrive in waterlogged conditions. It's at its best in full sun though it will tolerate some shade. Full shade leads to spindly growth and poor autumn colour.

No regular pruning is needed, although the removal of some of the lower branches will help show off the peeling bark.

Propagation

Very difficult for the home gardener and probably not worth attempting. The paperbark maple is also slow to raise from seed.

Uses in the garden

It is best planted near paths where you walk in winter for it's then that its peeling bark is most valued. Do not surround it with other plants that would hide the trunk.

Alternatives

There is no other maple quite like it. Others have interesting bark, but these fall into the 'snakebark' group with attractive streaking and mottling in various combinations of dark green, grey, white, purple and pink depending on the variety. I can recommend both *Acer davidii* and *A. grosseri* var. *hersii*.

Prunus
'Cheal's Weeping Cherry'

Small weeping cherry
Deciduous, to 12ft (3.6m)

A SMALL, strongly weeping tree, this is ideal for courtyards and small gardens as it grows slowly, stays compact and only reaches about 12ft (3.6m) in ten years. The branches arch quickly from the top of the stem and hang down vertically to the ground, creating a very attractive winter silhouette. Its main glory is its flowers which appear from mid to late spring and are large, dense and soft pink. There is some confusion between this and another variety. 'Kiku-shidare Sakura' is sometimes

The chief attraction of the paperbark maple (Acer griseum), as its common name suggests, is the handsome peeling bark, mahogany brown on the outside revealing the cinnamon-coloured trunk beneath.

sold as this plant, and vice versa, but this has branches which rise from the top of the trunk before arching widely and then weeping. The result is a much larger tree. Check the plant in the garden centre, or enclose a note to the nurseryman when ordering.

Cultivation

Any fertile soil suits it; poor soil will lead to weak growth and a generally tatty appearance. Full sun is almost essential though it will do reasonably well in the shade from a tall wall. Do not plant under overhead shade. In windy sites a stout stake is vital as the bulk of branches and foliage can catch in the wind and rock the roots. A little careful pruning to improve the shape is sometimes necessary.

Uses in the garden

This tree makes an ideal focal point for a courtyard or small garden. Don't crowd this variety with other plants or you won't be able to appreciate its shape.

Alternatives

The winter-flowering *Prunus subhirtella* has a number of weeping varieties with white or pink flowers. Here again the names are confused. Ask for 'Pendula' and you will probably get what is actually 'Pendula Rosea', with a neat habit and deep pink buds opening to paler flowers. The true 'Pendula' is rather larger.

Prunus serrula

Cherry with beautiful bark
Deciduous, to 15ft (4.5m)

Found growing wild in south-west China, it was first discovered by the plant hunting missionary, the Abbé Delavay, and first brought back to the west by the plant hunter 'Chinese' Wilson. It is a small tree reaching about 15ft (4.5m) in about ten years. Both the flowers and the foliage are unremarkable but the astonishing bark more than makes up for this. The colour of the bark varies from dark mahogany to pale chestnut, peeling slightly, with the breathing pores making rough horizontal streaks. The whole trunk of a mature tree gleams in the winter sunshine.

Cultivation

It is happy in almost any soil. Plant it where

it will get good light in the winter. No pruning is necessary though the removal of low branches will help make the best of the colouring of the trunk and cutting out twiggy growth higher up will help show off the branches as they develop their colour.

Propagation

It can be raised from the small black fruits, sown in a pot in the autumn and left outside, though the seedlings will be slow to appear.

Uses in the garden

This tree makes a fine winter feature. Its shade is not heavy so a wide range of plants can be planted beneath. This allows you to plant it in quite a prominent position.

Encourage visitors to rub the trunk as they pass as this will help it keep its shine. An annual scrub with soap and water is also very effective.

Alternatives

There are one or two other cherries with attractive bark such as *Prunus serrulata*, varieties of which have the bonus of attractive spring flowers.

Cultivation

It grows best in full sun and will be happy in most soils except those that are very dry or waterlogged. It must be staked well and plenty of compost or manure added when planting. Little pruning is usually required, but thinning of the branches may improve its appearance in the early years. This is not a strong rooting tree so staking, good soil preparation and watering are important in the first few years.

Uses in the garden

It is good as a specimen surrounded by pastel-shaded plants into which the delicate silvery branches can weep attractively. Clematis look delightful trained up into its branches and it is an essential constituent of a white garden.

Alternatives

There are two willows, *Salix alba* 'Sericea' and *S. exigua*, which make small silvery trees, but neither is weeping in form.

Laburnum × watereri
'Vossii'

Spectacular flowering tree
Deciduous, to 20ft (6m)

THIS LABURNUM is a hybrid between *L. alpinum*, which normally flowers in early summer with very long open, strings of flowers and *L. anagyroides* whose flowers are earlier but more densely clustered together in shorter strings. The variety 'Vossii' combines these characteristics, with its long strings of densely packed flowers. It was raised in Holland in the late 19th century. An excellent, rather upright, small to medium-sized tree, it reaches 20ft (6m) in 20 years and is suitable for all but the smallest gardens. Its bright, buttery-yellow scented flowers, which come in strings as long as 15in (38cm), are its chief, indeed its only, glory and are set off well by the dark foliage. They appear in late spring.

All laburnums produce seeds which are poisonous but only children who eat large quantities will be seriously harmed. This variety is almost sterile so very few seeds are produced. This also leads to the individual flowers lasting an especially long time.

The seed pods are rather unattractive and hang on to the tree for several months.

One nursery has produced what it calls 'Sheraton Cherries' by grafting flowering varieties on to trunks of *P. serrula*. The result is an extraordinary tree with lovely shining bark up to about 6ft (1.8m), a bulge where this meets the flowering variety and then quite different unremarkable bark in the crown of the tree. Discerning gardeners will eschew such monstrosities.

Pyrus salicifolia
'Pendula'

Silvery-leaved weeping pear
Deciduous, to 20ft (6m)

THIS VARIETY is an especially good form of a species which grows wild in south east Europe and western Asia. It is a slow-growing, mop-headed, weeping tree eventually reaching 20ft (6m), with silvery willow-like leaves and creamy-white flowers in mid spring, usually hidden by the leaves. The flowers are less important than the long display of almost white foliage and the attractive weeping form.

Acer palmatum 'Senkaki' has striking coral-red twigs, and bright yellow autumn foliage. It should be planted where its stems can be displayed to advantage.

Laburnums also tend to root poorly so good support is needed together with a position out of strong gales. They are not long-lived and may suddenly die at any time after about 20 years.

Cultivation

Any reasonable soil, including very limy soil, suits it well. It's best in full sun but it will also thrive in partial shade. Little or no pruning should be necessary.

Propagation

Plants in the garden centre are usually propagated by grafting and this is difficult for the home gardener. Plants raised from the few seeds produced will not necessarily be as good as their parent.

Uses in the garden

This is a specimen tree best used where it is not the only tree in the garden as its period of colour is short. It is a good host for climbers like clematis.

Alternatives

This beats all other laburnums. Another hybrid, 'Alford's Weeping', is sometimes recommended but rarely seen.

Acer palmatum
'Senkaki'

Tiny, slow-growing Japanese maple
Deciduous, to 6ft (1.8m)

THIS VERY small, elegant and relatively upright version of the Japanese maple was introduced from Japan around 1920. It reaches only 6ft (1.8m) in ten years. The leaves have a pinkish tinge when they open in spring and bright yellow autumn colour. The foliage only casts a light shade so many plants can be grown underneath. Perhaps its most striking feature is the coral-red twigs which shine brilliantly in the winter sunshine, especially against snow.

Cultivation

It grows best in a soil which is not too limy and is best planted where it is shaded from the full force of the summer sun which can scorch the leaves.

No pruning is usually necessary, though dead and diseased wood should always be removed. Coral spot disease infects dead

wood first and then spreads to healthy growth. Small raised spots of a dark coral colour on dead shoots give it away. If you see the signs, prune out infected shoots and seal the cuts with a pruning compound.

Propagation

Very difficult for the home gardener and probably not worth attempting.

Uses in the garden

Plant this tree where it will get sun for at least part of the day in winter and where you will be able to see the winter twigs.

Plants sometimes appear in garden centres with the name 'Sango Kaku'. You may get 'Senkaki' if you buy this or you may get a plant with much redder twigs. Either way you get a wonderful plant.

Alternatives

There are none apart from 'Sango Kaku'.

Cornus kousa
var. chinensis

All-seasons specimen tree
Deciduous, to 20ft (6m)

THIS LOVELY small tree was introduced to America from Hupeh in China in 1907 and first grown in the UK at Kew in 1910. It is rather bushy in growth, eventually reaching 20ft (6m) in height after about 30 years. Initial growth is slow and it may not flower until four or five years after planting. The inconspicuous flowers appear in early summer and stand up from the horizontal branches. Although the flowers themselves are not showy, each cluster is surrounded by four large creamy white, petal-like leaves which turn pink as they age and show up from quite a distance. Later in the season the foliage turns an astonishing orangy-red and is held on the tree for an exceptionally long period.

Cultivation

This dogwood is happy on most soils except very limey ones. It thrives most happily in acid conditions and a rich and well-drained soil suits it best. It prefers light shade but is generally tolerant of all but fully shaded sites. No pruning is necessary.

Propagation

It is not easy to propagate but low-growing shoots can be layered and soft cuttings can be taken in mid summer.

Uses in the garden

With its two seasons of interest this tree is a good choice as the only one in a small garden. In larger situations it makes a fine feature in a mixed border. Its preference for acid soil and partial shade makes it a fine plant for the woodland garden with ferns, primulas, dwarf rhododendrons and other plants liking similar conditions.

Alternatives

A hybrid between *C. kousa* and *C. capitata* called 'Norman Haddon' is pink rather than creamy white and usually retains at least some leaves all winter. It's more difficult to find in garden centres though it is stocked by specialist nurseries. *C. nuttalii* grows to at least twice the height of *C. kousa*.

Salix caprea
'Pendula'

Weeping Kilmarnock willow
Deciduous, to 6–7ft
(1.8–2.1m)

THE KILMARNOCK willow is a weeping version of the familiar pussy willow. It makes a small, neat, weeping tree eventually reaching a maximum of 10ft (3m) in height but taking many years to do so. Specimens of 6–7ft (1.8–2.1m) are far more common. The young stems are purplish in colour and all the branches hang down vertically to the ground making a

waterfall of silvery and yellow catkins in the late winter.

Cultivation

It is easy to grow in full sun in fertile soil that is not too dry. Usually no pruning is necessary except to correct an imbalance in the distribution of branches. Shoots growing from the trunk should be cut off flush.

Propagation

Hardwood cuttings can be taken in late autumn and inserted in a sheltered spot outside in the garden. They should root by spring and can be moved to their final position in the autumn. Train a single shoot up a stout stake and remove the top at the height from which you wish it to weep; 4–6ft (1.2–1.8m) is about right. Retain the stake for support.

Uses in the garden

It is best used as a focal point in a small garden especially by a water feature.

Cornus kousa var. chinensis makes a bushy small tree, whose chief glory is the profusion of starry creamy-white bracts in spring.

There are many varieties of crab apple but *Malus 'Golden Hornet'* offers white spring flowers, bright golden clusters of fruit and an attractive rounded head of branches.

This Lawson's cypress (Chamaecyparis lawsoniana 'Lanei') is particularly elegant with its golden colour and neat pyramidal shape.

Alternatives

Salix caprea has male and female catkins on separate plants. The Kilmarnock willow is a male variety but there is also a female one called 'Weeping Sally' that has silvery catkins but is difficult to find.

Betula pendula
'Tristis'

Elegant weeping birch
Deciduous, to 20ft (6m)

THIS GRACEFUL, almost ethereal, weeping birch is grown for its elegant weeping habit, its shape and its attractive white bark. Its yellow autumn colour is good but not spectacular. Quick-growing, though not making a huge specimen, it should reach about 20ft (6m) in ten years and then slow down. Like all birches, it casts a relatively light shade which is particularly welcome in smaller gardens. Some gardeners might complain that it doesn't have flowers or colourful foliage, but it really doesn't need them.

Cultivation

It is happy on all but the wettest soils. Ensure that a good leader develops to be certain of a well-shaped specimen; this leader may need a little support. No pruning is usually required – in fact the more you prune it, the more likely you are to ruin the shape of the tree.

Propagation

Very difficult for the home gardener and probably not worth attempting. Seedlings will not necessarily produce similar trees.

Uses in the garden

It is best set against a dark background where the white bark shows up most effectively. This lovely birch makes a splendid focal point as its shape is very attractive even in winter.

Alternatives

There is also a much smaller weeping birch, *Betula pendula* 'Youngii', which is useful for very small plots. But its growth is rather compressed and hummock-like. The Swedish Birch, 'Dalecarlica', is more vigorous and only slightly weeping but has attractive deeply cut leaves.

Malus
'Golden Hornet'

White-flowered crab apple
Deciduous, 18ft (5.4m)

RAISED BY Waterers nursery, this tree was given an Award of Merit by the Royal Horticultural Society in 1949 and a First Class Certificate in 1961. It is a white-flowered crab apple flowering in mid spring, reaching about 18ft (5.4m) in ten years with a rounded head of branches. The flowers appear in spring and are followed in autumn by generous quantities of bright yellow, round or egg-shaped fruits in clusters of three or four. They often stay on the tree until well into the winter months.

'Golden Hornet' and other varieties of crab apple are now available grafted on to rootstocks which keep them much more dwarf than usual.

This variety is a good pollinator for eating and cooking apples and its long flowering period means that only one tree is needed.

Cultivation

'Golden Hornet' is happy in most soil conditions but dislikes waterlogged soil. Plenty of sunshine gives the best fruit colour but a little shade is not too detrimental. Dead, diseased and rubbing branches should be removed and if the centre gets too congested, a few branches can be removed to let the sun in to ripen the fruit.

Propagation

Most of the plants on sale are grafted and this is a highly skilled job requiring special training. Plants raised from pips will produce unpredictable results and may not fruit well.

Uses in the garden

This is a valuable tree for all but very small gardens where the two seasons of interest are most useful.

Alternatives

The orange- and scarlet-fruited 'John Downie' makes better jelly but is more susceptible to scab and mildew than most varieties. 'Wintergold' retains its fruit especially well into the winter.

Chamaecyparis lawsoniana
'Lanei'

Slender Lawson's cypress
Evergreen, to 30ft (9m)

R AISED BY Lane's Nurseries of Berkhamsted in Hertfordshire about 1938, this narrow-growing, upright Lawson's cypress is of a most elegant shape, broader at the base but still neat. It eventually reaches 30ft (9m) but takes as many years. The sprays of foliage are spreading, rather lacy, golden yellow above and greener below, giving a mottled effect. It is one of the brightest yellow conifers.

Cultivation

It thrives best in a rich soil. Although it will tolerate poor conditions it will grow less well and may tend to lose its lower branches, spoiling the shape of the mature tree. It is happy in slight but not dense shade. No pruning is usually required.

Propagation

Cuttings 2–3in (5–7.5cm) long can be taken in a frost-free frame or greenhouse in late autumn or a cold frame in early spring. Remove a sliver of bark from the base of the cutting before dipping it in a hormone rooting powder and insert four or five in a 3-in (7.5-cm) pot of cuttings compost or in the soil in the base of the frame. Make sure they never dry out. They should be rooted in late spring or early summer.

Uses in the garden

This variety makes a splendid focal point in all but the smallest gardens and associates well with heathers, other conifers and foliage shrubs of all sorts. Dark-leaved berberis and elder along with silver foliage, make good companions and dark-flowered clematis look lovely trained into mature specimens. Its slow initial growth rate coupled with its eventual stature can make it difficult to position well at first. When sited with its eventual size in mind, as it should be, care must be taken to ensure that it's not smothered in its early stages.

Betula jacquemontii, like B. 'Jermyns', has attractive pale-coloured bark and a fairly narrow upright form. Ideally both should be planted against a dark background to set off the silvery bark.

Alternatives

Other good yellow varieties include 'Golden King' with bronzed autumn colour and 'Stewartii' with golden foliage.

Betula
'Jermyns'
Ghostly white-stemmed birch
Deciduous, to 30ft (9m)

INTRODUCED BY Hilliers in the mid-1970s, this plant was originally received by them from Sweden in 1933. The bark of this variety is almost unbelievable, being as pure a white as any available. The tree has a fairly narrow, upright habit and should reach about 30ft (9m) in ten years, but like most birches will slow down in later life. It casts only light shade. In spring the long catkins are also very attractive. This is not a long-lived tree and at the age of around 50, it may suddenly die for no apparent reason.

Cultivation

It is happy in a wide range of conditions although it grows poorly in waterlogged soil. It is best planted in full sun, though it grows well in some shade, especially if cast from the side rather than from above. Some gardeners scrub the bark occasionally so it really shines. No pruning is usually necessary though the lower branches may be removed to reveal more of the white trunk.

Propagation

Very difficult for the home gardener and probably not worth attempting. Seedlings will not necessarily produce similar trees.

Uses in the garden

The shining white bark is best set against a dark background such as an evergreen hedge so that the contrast shows off the bark to advantage.

Alternatives

There are a number of other birches with outstanding white bark. 'Grayswood Ghost' is very similar but the catkins are shorter and less showy. Both *Betula utilis* and *B. jacquemontii* are often seen and these two are fine trees. The former has rather creamy bark, and the latter develops areas of brown bark which peels back to reveal the white underneath.

SHRUBS

S HRUBS ARE the plant features that give a garden or border its shape and set its style. They are fundamental to the success of your garden and your enjoyment of it at its most attractive – and when it's not quite at its best.

They define the structure of the garden in a soft and natural way which cannot be done by walls and fences and represent solid, lasting features around which smaller and more transient plantings can be developed.

Shrubs also feature in other categories in this survey of the best of all garden plants. In particular they're to be found amongst the foliage plants, but also amongst the scented plants, connoisseurs' plants, and wall shrubs.

Rhododendrons and other acid-loving plants have, sadly, been left out of my selection. This was a difficult decision for although I recognize how popular they are amongst gardeners who have soil conditions to suit them, over large parts of the country it's impossible to grow a decent rhododendron except in a container. The shrubs I've chosen are those with a more universal appeal.

Shrubs can be grown for their foliage, flowers, fruits, autumn colour, coloured stems and general habit. All these features are represented in the selection. One or two of the shrubs may reach tree-like proportions if left to do so. Some of them are single-season plants, though most give more than one season of colour value.

Rhus typhina
'Laciniata'

Autumn-tinted specimen plant
Deciduous, to 10ft (3m)

T HIS IS THE cut-leaved form of a species that grows wild in eastern North America and has been cultivated in the UK since the 17th century. It is a sparsely branched, widely spreading, deciduous shrub with large deeply cut leaves up to 18in (45cm) long. In autumn these leaves turn a raging fiery red and yellow. This is a female form and knobbly, but not showy, rather conical flower heads appear at the end of the branches and remain over the winter, giving the appearance of a giant hat-stand. If there's a male nearby, hairy red fruits may follow. It has more than a tendency to sucker, especially if cut back hard as suggested and if the roots are damaged. This cut-leaved variety may occasionally revert to the ordinary form. It also comes into leaf rather late in the spring. The sap can irritate the skin of some people.

Cultivation

It is happy in most soils and situations. To encourage the largest foliage on plants of manageable size, cut back to ground level or to a low framework in spring. If a larger shrub is needed, leave a few years between doses of this treatment and cut back to a higher framework.

Propagation

Suckers can be detached from the parent plant and transplanted to their new home in spring or autumn.

Uses in the garden

Although it can be used as a free-standing specimen, it is perhaps better in the back of a mixed border where the savage pruning is less necessary. It is also good in front of other trees.

Alternatives

The plain-leaved form is less attractive but the autumn colour is redder.

Forsythia
'Lynwood'

Reliable winter flowerer
Hardy, to 8ft (2.4m)

O VER THE years some poor forms of this variety have appeared in garden centres. The Clonal Stock Selection Scheme set out to find the best and a specially selected version now carries the suffix LA, being the initials of the research station at Long Ashton where the trials and the selection were carried out. It's well worth looking for. 'Lynwood' was discovered in a garden in Northern Ireland and introduced in 1935. A tough and easy-to-grow deciduous shrub, with sadly unremarkable plain green foliage, it carries large, rich yellow flowers all along the straw-coloured branches in early spring. It reaches about 8ft (2.4m) in height.

Cultivation

It grows happily in most soils and in full sun or part shade. The more shade it has, the more open the growth and the fewer the flowers. Prune back all shoots that have flowered to a point where a strong new growth is emerging. Remove one or two older shoots entirely to encourage new growth, but not every year. Old, untidy plants can be cut back to about 6in (15cm) in spring and will soon re-grow.

Propagation

It is not difficult to raise from 3–4-in (7.5–10-cm) tip cuttings taken in mid summer or 9-in (23-cm) hardwood cuttings, which should be taken in late autumn.

Uses in the garden

Plant this shrub where it can be appreciated in winter – near a path, for example, and with an evergreen shrub or fence to provide a background to the flowers.

Alternatives

Other good varieties include 'Beatrix Farrand' which makes a denser bush with exceptionally large nodding flowers, each with a purple throat, and the very vigorous 'Karl Sax'. *Forsythia viridissima* 'Bronxensis' is a dwarf twiggy form that prefers a reasonably well-drained soil.

Erica carnea
'Springwood White'

Vigorous winter-flowering heather
Hardy, to 6–9in (15–23cm)

SOME YEARS ago the botanical name of this plant was changed to *Erica herbacea* 'Springwood White' and it will be increasingly labelled and listed with this name. The original plant was found on Monte Carreggio in Italy by the late Mrs Ralph Walker of Springwood, near Stirling. It was named at Wisley and has won many awards, the first being in 1930. It is a pure white winter-flowering heather with chocolate-coloured pollen peeping out of the flower. The foliage is apple green and it's

one of the most vigorous winter-flowering varieties, reaching 6–9in (15–23cm) in height and spreading widely, making a good weed-suppressing cover once established. The flower spikes are long and plants keep flowering from around mid winter, often until well into spring .

Cultivation

This very tough and tolerant plant is at its best in neutral to acid soil, but grows in limy soils unlike most heathers. It seems happy in sand or clay as long as both have been improved with peat. It thrives in the cold and gives its best in partially shady conditions although long, hard winters will take their toll. Mulching with peat or bark is sensible too. Clip over in spring after flowering otherwise new growth will come only from the shoot tips and as a result the plants will soon become horribly straggly with bare centres.

Propagation

Cuttings about 2–3-in (5–7.5-cm) long root in early summer in a lime-free compost.

Uses in the garden

This is a vital winter garden plant for use with other winter heathers, or with summer heathers in a heather garden, in a raised bed or with other small plants and bulbs near the house.

Erica carnea 'Springwood White', unlike most heathers, is happy in improved limey soils and will do best in slight shade.

Rosa 'Iceberg' produces its glorious flowers all over the bush, not just on top. Light pruning will help to promote flowering.

Alternatives

Of the many other varieties available I would select 'Springwood Pink', 'Vivellii' with deep pink flowers and dark bronzy foliage, and 'Winter Beauty' with pink flowers, which is the first to bloom.

Rosa
'Iceberg'

White-flowered floribunda rose
Hardy, to 4–5ft (1.2–1.5m)

RAISED IN Germany in 1958, this is a cross between 'Robin Hood' and 'Virgo' made by Kordes, who is still introducing good varieties. It is a white-flowered floribunda rose whose flowers appear in large numbers all around the bush, not just on the top, but have very little scent. The foliage is a fresh green shade. Growth is rather lax and spreading so the plant makes a bush about 4–5ft (1.2–1.5m) high depending on the type of pruning. The stems are almost thornless.

Cultivation

It seems to thrive on a wide variety of soils but like most roses appreciates generous treatment. It grows best in sun, but seems to do well in a little shade. 'Iceberg' is best pruned lightly to create the most shapely bush with plenty of flowers at all levels. Cut back to 14–16in (35–40cm) in spring. Mildew is a big problem but regular spraying with a fungicide containing benomyl (e.g. ICI Benlate) will keep it at bay.

Propagation

Cuttings 3–4in (7.5–10cm) long can be rooted in a propagator in mid summer or alternatively 9-in (23-cm) hardwood cuttings can be set outside in early winter.

Uses in the garden

It makes a good hedge or a good specimen shrub that looks well in a small group in a border, or can be given a bed of its own.

Alternatives

For another white rose 'Margaret Merrill' is the only option – it has slightly fewer flowers, a wonderful scent and very dark, slightly reddish foliage. It also needs slightly better treatment. In a mixed border, the shrub roses are best.

Rosa
'Canary Bird'

Back-of-border rose
Hardy, to 6ft (1.8m)

THIS IS A selected form of *Rosa xanthina* var. *spontanea*, introduced from China in around 1908. A tall, slightly ungainly rose, it has graceful lateral shoots arching from its branches that mask the stiff habit and create an attractive look. The foliage is neat and small, almost fernlike, with a slightly greyish hue. The big single flowers, about 2in (5cm) across and of a deep canary yellow, line the branches in mid spring. Occasional flowers sometimes appear in the autumn.

Cultivation

It is a little fussier than many roses, demanding a well-drained, fairly fertile soil and full sun to thrive. It's probably best left unpruned but if pruning is necessary to keep it in bounds or to improve the habit, do so immediately after flowering. Occasionally, for no apparent reason, branches die out. These should be cut out leaving no dead wood behind and the plant will then recover and continue to thrive. A fertile soil and regular mulching with organic matter will help to prevent this problem but it may spoil the effect of plants grown in a hedge. This problem is also less likely to affect plants grown from cuttings than those budded on to a different rootstock as most roses are.

Propagation

Either 3–4-in (7.5–10-cm) cuttings can be taken in summer and rooted in a propagator, or 9-in (23-cm) cuttings taken in early winter and rooted in a sheltered spot outside.

Uses in the garden

A fine specimen plant for the back of the mixed border, it will support a less vigorous, small-flowered clematis well. It is occasionally seen as an informal hedge.

Alternatives

There is a number of other very pretty early-flowering roses in this group. The even deeper coloured 'Helen Knight' is lovely but more difficult to find in nurseries, as are the creamy-coloured 'Albert Edwards' and the smaller-flowered white 'Cantabridgensis'.

Cotoneaster
'Cornubia'

Spreading, scarlet-berried evergreen
Hardy, to 20ft (6m)

THIS IS A hybrid raised at Exbury Gardens in Hampshire by the late Lionel de Rothschild around 1930. Its parents are probably varieties of *Cotoneaster frigidus* and *C. salicifolius*. A tall, evergreen shrub, it sometimes reaches 20ft (6m) with spreading growth and long narrow glossy foliage. Large clusters of white flowers appear in early summer followed by generous bunches of brilliant red fruits which weigh down the branches.

Rosa 'Canary Bird' has handsome, bright yellow single flowers and neat, fern-like foliage. It will make an attractive informal hedge.

Cultivation

It is happy in all but very chalky soils and in full sun or half shade. Pruning is not usually required though a little thoughtful reduction in size may eventually be necessary in many gardens.

The only problem, apart from birds eating the berries, is fireblight. This is a bacterial disease that most frequently attacks hawthorn hedges and also apples and pears. The symptoms are wilting blossoms and shoot tips followed by die-back, stained wood and eventually the death of the plant. It also attacks ornamental trees and shrubs and some cotoneasters are especially susceptible. Fortunately 'Cornubia' is less susceptible than most but in rural areas infection is possible.

Propagation

It roots well from partially ripe cuttings taken in early summer and rooted in a heated propagator.

Uses in the garden

It is useful in the back of the border as it makes a fine background to other plants and can be treated as the equivalent of a small, well-furnished tree.

Alternatives

A variety of similar size and habit but with yellow fruits is 'Exburiensis'. Smaller varieties with red fruits include 'John Waterer' and *C. salicifolius* var. *floccosus*.

Ribes sanguineum 'Pulborough Scarlet' is an easy-to-grow shrub with clusters of deep red flowers covering the branches in spring. It needs some pruning to give the best display.

Magnolia × soulangiana

Exotic specimen shrub
Deciduous, to 15ft (4.5m)

THIS HYBRID between *M. denudata* and *M. liliflora*, themselves good garden plants, was raised in France 1826 by a retired cavalry officer from Napoleon's army. It is a large, openly branched, widely spreading shrub carrying large goblet-shaped flowers on the bare branches in mid spring, giving it a rather exotic air. The flowers are white inside and flushed with purplish pink outside. It can eventually reach 15ft (4.5m) in height and breadth. It flowers at a younger age than many magnolias but still may not flower until two or three years after planting.

Cultivation

It thrives on clay and most other types of soil but is not happy in very limey conditions. Shelter from the early morning sun will protect the flowers from thawing too rapidly and turning brown. No pruning is usually required.

Propagation

Low branches can be pegged down into improved soil in early summer and will be ready for severing and planting elsewhere by the following spring.

Uses in the garden

It makes a very attractive specimen shrub that needs plenty of space to spread its branches widely.

Alternatives

'Alba Superba' is pure white with a more upright habit; 'Lennei' flowers later with a rosy flush to the outside of the petals; 'Rustica Rubra' is a richer colour.

Ribes sanguineum
'Pulborough Scarlet'

Reliable winter-flowerer
Hardy, to 8ft (2.4m)

THIS IS A selected variety of a species that was first discovered in western North America in 1793 and introduced into western Europe in 1817. It is a stiff and strong-growing, very hardy and tol-

erant deciduous shrub with shoots that sweep sideways at first, then turn upright. It flowers in early spring, with hanging clusters of deep red flowers all along the growth made the previous year. Some people notice a rather unpleasant catty smell from the flowers.

Cultivation

It is happy in most soils except where it's very dry or very wet, and in most situations, although it prefers just a little shade. Regular pruning is essential. Some gardeners cut the whole plant to the ground after flowering each spring but the removal of about a third of the shoots, the oldest, at ground level or above a low young shoot will ensure that growth is not too strong. Very strong growth after heavy pruning results in wider spaces between the flowers and thus a less effective display.

Propagation

Either 3–4-in (7.5–10-cm) cuttings can be taken in early summer or 9-in (23-cm) hardwood cuttings can be taken in early winter.

Uses in the garden

A good specimen plant for the mixed border, it will be dominant in late winter and

One of the finest specimen shrubs, Magnolia × soulangiana *carries its large goblet-shaped flowers on bare branches in spring.*

early spring but if then cut back hard will leave a view through to other plants later in spring and early summer.

Alternatives

There are a number of other good varieties such as 'King Edward VII' which grows rather less strongly but is a similar colour. The flowers of 'Splendens' are paler and come in larger clusters and 'Tydeman's White' is white-flowered and a little less vigorous. 'Brocklebankii' is much less vigorous and has pink flowers and yellow foliage, although this can easily scorch and discolour in full sun.

An upright evergreen, Mahonia 'Charity' has impressive large holly-like leaves and strings of small yellow flowers in winter.

Cytisus
'Allgold'

Striking yellow spring-flowerer, Hardy to 5ft (1.5m)

THIS IS A hybrid raised in Holland and originally derived from *C. purgans* and *C. multiflorus*. A short-lived, rather wiry, almost leafless shrub with green stems, it makes a twiggy bush up to 5ft (1.5m) high. In late spring it's covered in golden-yellow pea-flowers which line the branches, making a yellow fireball. This display is its most stunning asset although the spiky structure and green twigs are interesting features for the rest of the year.

However, it usually needs replacing after ten years, and has a tendency not to shoot after pruning into old wood.

Cultivation

It is happy in most soils except where waterlogged or excessively limey, but demands full sun. Trimming after flowering helps keep the plant bushy – but never cut into old, dark wood.

Propagation

It roots well in a heated propagator from cuttings taken in early summer. The shoots will appear to have almost no leaves but they will still root and you can get quite a few in a 3-in (7.5-cm) pot of compost.

Uses in the garden

Use this shrub where a bold splash is needed; a single plant in a mixed border can be very dramatic.

Alternatives

There are a number of related varieties in different colours. 'C. E. Pearson' is creamy yellow with a crimson flush, 'Albus' is pure white, and 'Zealandia' is lilac and cream.

Mahonia
'Charity'

Evergreen winter flowerer
Hardy, to 6ft (1.8m)

SELECTED AT Russell's Nursery in Surrey in the early 1950's, 'Charity' is a hybrid between *M. japonica* and *M. lomarii- folia*. An upright evergreen shrub, it has im-

Camellia *'Donation' is one of the most exotic shrubs with its clear pink double flowers in early spring.*

pressive long leaves divided into pairs of holly-like leaflets. In late autumn and into winter the small yellow flowers are carried in long strings up to 12 in (30cm) in length springing from the tops of the shoots and surrounded by the ruff of leaves. Birds can ruin the display by pecking off the buds even before they open. It has no scent.

Cultivation

Although tolerant of most soils except those which are dry and limey, a fairly well-drained but not dry soil with plenty of organic matter seems to suit it best. Full sun or light shade are ideal, but full shade ruins the stout stance of the plant. Pruned just below the flowering head after flowering to encourage branching.

Propagation

This plant can be grown from cuttings taken in early summer but they are so slow to root that success can be elusive.

Uses in the garden

These are ideal as specimen shrubs or at the back of the mixed border. It is important to place them so that they will be seen in winter when they are flowering. If not pruned, the resultant bare stems will need screening by lower plants.

Alternatives

M. lomariifolia is rather taller and has much better foliage but is more tender. Other good hybrids include 'Lionel Fortescue', which is taller and has especially long strings of flowers, and 'Winter Sun' which has more erect, particularly well-scented flower spikes.

Camellia
'Donation'

Exotic evergreen

Hardy, to 6ft (1.8m)

THIS IS A variety of *Camellia × williamsii*, a hybrid between *Camellia japonica* and *C. saluensis*. It was raised between the wars by Colonel Stephenson Clarke at his garden at Borde Hill in Sussex.

A useful border filler, Senecio 'Sunshine' makes a rounded evergreen bush covered with bright yellow daisies in summer.

It is an evergreen shrub of upright growth reaching about 6ft (1.8m) in ten years. The foliage is deep green and glossy, and in late winter and early spring there are semi-double flowers of a clear orchid pink with slightly darker veins.

Cultivation

Acid soil is essential to the growth of this exceptional shrub, and a soil which remains moist during the hottest days of summer, though not waterlogged, is the almost unattainable ideal. Camellias also require light shade to give their best but are better in deeper shade than in full sun. No pruning is usually required though mature plants may need their shape improving and can also be reduced in size by careful removal of the longer shoots at a point within the main bulk of the plant.

Bud drop is a well-known problem with camellias and there are two popular explanations. The first is frost, or rather thaw. The theory is that it doesn't matter if the flower buds freeze, but if they thaw too quickly, then the buds drop off. The solution to this problem is to plant the camellia in a position facing the evening sun or away from the sun.

The second theory is one that I have a little more sympathy with. In late summer the camellia is forming the buds which will produce flowers the following spring. If the plant suffers from a dry spell at this stage then the stalk which joins the bud to the shoot does not develop properly. Nothing appears amiss until the bud starts to expand prior to flowering and at this stage the stress is too much for the weak stem and the bud falls off. The remedy to this problem is a moisture-retentive soil, mulching with organic matter and watering in summer and early autumn in dry spells, especially on well-drained soils.

I suspect that in many cases a combination of the two factors could be at work. The extra stress of rapid thawing is sometimes the last straw which provokes a bout of bud dropping when the buds have already been weakened by drought.

Camellias are actually very hardy plants. Although when they were first grown in this country they were thought to be tender and were kept in conservatories, this has proved quite unnecessary.

Propagation

Cuttings consisting of just two leaf joints can

be taken in mid summer. Trim below the lower leaf and remove the leaf, and trim above the upper leaf. Remove a sliver of bark from the base of the stem opposite the bud, treat with hormone rooting powder and place three cuttings in a 5-in (12.5-cm) pot containing acid compost, often called ericaceous compost.

Uses in the garden

A fine specimen shrub, it can even be trained flat on a wall in a small garden if necessary. It's also a fine plant for a large container but demands constant watering in high summer.

Alternatives

Of the many other remarkably fine camellias available I would also recommend the darker pink 'Debbie', the deep red 'Adolphe Audusson' and the white single 'Cornish Snow'.

not waterlogged, a well-drained soil is best. Full sun produces the most colourful display. Cut out about a quarter of the growth at around ground level in early spring to encourage the production of new growth from low down. Plants can become floppy if not pruned regularly in spring.

Propagation

Take cuttings 3–4in (7.5–10cm) long in early summer and root them in a propagator.

Uses in the garden

This reliable shrub will create an accent at the front of the border or a focal point in a grey foliage border or dry garden.

Alternatives

Other available senecios seem to be less hardy and so less suitable for most gardens.

Hypericum
'Hidcote'

Long-flowering evergreen
Hardy, to 5ft (1.3m)

T HIS PLANT WAS noticed in the garden at Hidcote Manor in Gloucestershire and introduced in 1950. It is a broadly spreading shrub, virtually evergreen, and reaching about 5ft (1.3m) in height. The dark green foliage is the ideal background for the huge buttercup-like flowers, up to 3in (7.5cm) across. They appear from early summer well into the autumn.

Cultivation

A tolerant plant, it thrives in all but dry soils and is best in a little shade. It still grows

Senecio
'Sunshine'

Evergreen border filler
Hardy, to 3–4ft (0.9–1.2m)

T HERE HAS been some confusion over the name of this plant and for many years it was known as *Senecio greyii*. 'Sunshine' is actually a hybrid between *S. greyii* and the smaller, more compact *S. compactus*. It is a rather lax evergreen shrub with silvery grey foliage, making a rounded plant reaching 3–4ft (90cm–1.2m) in about ten years. Pruning can dramatically influence the size and look of the plant. The bright yellow daisy flowers appear in early summer, often for many weeks.

Cultivation

Although it is happy in many soils that are

The handsome, large yellow flowers of Hypericum *'Hidcote' start appearing in early summer and continue until autumn. A broad-spreading semi-evergreen, it is ideal for the mixed border.*

Lupinus arboreus

Vigorous tree lupin

Hardy evergreen,
to 6ft (1.8m)

Tᴴɪs ᴛʀᴇᴇ lupin grows wild on the Californian coast and was introduced to Europe in about 1793. It is a quick-growing, well-branched, largely evergreen shrub reaching 6ft (1.8m) in just a few years but often dying shortly afterwards. The leaves are recognizably those of a lupin, as are the slightly scented flowers. They appear throughout the summer and are usually sharp yellow in colour but seed-raised plants may be paler yellow, cream, lilac and a number of other rather dirty-looking shades.

Cultivation

It grows best in full sun in a well-drained soil. Self-sown seedlings will usually appear to take over from the parent plant when it dies. No regular pruning is usually required but branches are sometimes broken by the weight of winter snow and these will need tidying up in spring.

In recent years a new species of aphid has arrived in the UK from America. The lupin aphid must be the largest variation of the greenfly I've ever seen and the speed with which it multiplies is quite astonishing. It spends mild winters feeding on tree lupins, crippling the plants before they even start to grow in spring. The lupin aphid is easily killed by an insecticide containing pirimi-carb (e.g. ICI Rapid) but seems to reinfect quickly so must be controlled regularly.

Propagation

Tree lupins are easily propagated and seed sown in spring and treated like a half-hardy annual will produce shapely plants which may flower in their first year and will certainly bloom well the following spring.

Uses in the garden

The tree lupin is ideal for new gardens as it makes a substantial plant quickly and so gives an air of maturity and prevents the garden from looking bare while the more permanent plants become established.

Alternatives

There is nothing quite like this delightful and valuable. shrub.

The tree lupin (Lupinus arboreus) is a handsome, if short-lived, shrub with attractive lupin-like flowers in summer. It needs full sun and a well-drained soil to make the best growth.

reasonably well in full sun or rather more shade. Remove a quarter to a third of shoots at ground level each year to stimulate new growth from the base. The whole plant can also be cut back to the ground in spring if necessary. In severe winters there may be a little die-back but regrowth is rapid.

Propagation

Take cuttings 3–4in (7.5–10cm) long in early summer.

Uses in the garden

A fine specimen shrub for the mixed border, it also makes a good informal hedge.

Alternatives

'Rowallane' is often said to be a slightly finer variety with flowers of an especially attractive shape, but it is noticeably more tender than 'Hidcote'. A new version of 'Hidcote' with gold-splashed foliage should be available next year.

CLIMBERS

THE RANGE OF climbers available is extraordinarily large, especially when you consider the huge numbers of climbing roses, clematis and ivies. This enormous range gives you all the opportunities you need to add that vital extra dimension to the garden.

Climbers can be trained up walls and fences, pergolas and pillars or they can be allowed to scramble through shrubs and trees – as they do in the wild. It's interesting that the reason why roses have thorns is not to stop animals eating them, but to support themselves as they scramble up through shrubs and trees.

The great thing about all climbers is that they allow you to clothe vertical surfaces and to garden towards the sky, increasing the diversity of your planting and giving you a better chance to create an attractive garden. Of course growing climbers imposes special disciplines. Pruning is often especially necessary to keep the more vigorous ones within bounds and also to prevent even those of modest growth from giving their attention to neighbouring shrubs which could well do without it.

Clematis
'Bill McKenzie'

Deciduous twiner,
Hardy, to 13ft (4m)

THE ORIGIN OF this plant is a little confused and the naming of 'Bill McKenzie' and a number of similar plants like *Clematis orientalis* and *C. tangutica* is also bewildering. Many of the plants you find in garden centres are likely to be wrongly named and you should never raise any from seed as the results will be unpredictable. Get your 'Bill McKenzie' from a clematis specialist. A deciduous climber reaching up to 13ft (4m) in height, it supports itself by twining its leaf stems firmly around any convenient supports. The lemon-yellow, four-petalled flowers are thick and waxy and open widely. They appear from mid summer until well into the autumn and are followed by large silky seed heads. Flowers and seed heads are often

seen together. This really is a vigorous plant – it can grow as much as 12ft (3.6m) in a season and that means there's a lot of foliage to cope with. Older plants will need a little thinning at pruning time and it pays to give the shoots some guidance or they may set off determinedly in the wrong direction.

Cultivation

This is a tough plant without the susceptibility to wilt disease that finally destroys so many large-flowered hybrids. It tolerates a wider variety of soils than most. In the coldest areas some plants may suffer in severe winters but a well-drained soil will usually see them through. Hard pruning in spring will keep this vigorous plant within reasonable bounds and cutting back to a short framework about 18in (45cm) high is usually necessary.

Propagation

Plants can be raised from seed but they'll usually be inferior to the parent so it's better to layer shoots as then you get an exact replica. In winter, scoop out a depression about 4in (10cm) deep, lay a convenient stem in the dip and put a stone on the top. Finish off neatly with soil. By the following autumn you can cut the rooted shoot from its parent and plant it in its permanent position in the garden.

Uses in the garden

Wires are needed if the plant is to be trained on a wall but it usually looks better scrambling through a large shrub or small tree.

Alternatives

'Orange Peel', is almost the same except that the flowers are darker. *C. tangutica* can

Clematis *'Bill McKenzie' is one of the later-flowering clematis – from mid summer until autumn – in which the attractive yellow flowers and the silky seed heads are to be seen at the same time on the plant.*

be good but varies unpredictably. Other small-flowered, spring-flowering plants are *C. montana*, especially the variety 'Tetra-rose' with large purplish-pink flowers. 'Elizabeth' is paler pink with a slight vanilla scent. The blue *C. macropetala* is almost as good.

Clematis
'Vyvyan Pennell'

Deciduous twiner

Hardy, to 10ft (3m)

THIS IS a hybrid between the later-flowering, semi-double purple 'Daniel Deronda' and the long-flowering deep blue 'Beauty of Worcester'. It is a very free-flowering variety with double flowers appearing in late spring and early summer. The outer petals are large, even and lavender in colour with a paler central stripe while the smaller central rosette has a bluish tinge. This is one of the more sturdy and vigorous varieties in the group. One of the great things about 'Vyvyan Pennell' is that in late summer, a couple of months after the main flush of double flowers has faded, there's a second flush of very attractive single flowers. Like most large-flowered types it is liable to unpredictable and incurable attack from wilt but otherwise has few faults.

Cultivation

A heavy soil should suit it best but a light soil which has been much improved will do very well. It prefers a cool root run so shade from a small shrub or planting alongside paving is usually recommended. Cutting out dead wood and trimming back the dead shoots to a pair of fat buds in spring is usually sufficient pruning, and if you don't get round to it the plant won't suffer unduly. Separate the shoots and train them evenly over the area to be covered.

Propagation

Layering (as described under 'Bill McKenzie') is the best method of propagation.

Uses in the garden

This clematis is good on a sunny wall and also scrambling through a large shrub.

Alternatives

Other large-flowered hybrids to consider

are the familiar, striped 'Nelly Moser' and the deep blue 'Lasurstern' amongst the late spring types, and the rich purple 'Jackmanii' and the pale blue 'Perle d'Azur' amongst the summer and autumn types.

Clematis *'Vyvyan Pennell' is a very free-flowering double variety which often produces a second flush of blooms in the autumn.*

Eccremocarpus scaber

Long-flowering climber

Half-hardy annual, to 10ft (3m)

THIS VIGOROUS deciduous plant is known as the Chilean glory vine. It clings by the tendrils at the tips of its leaves. The flowers are tubular and orangy-yellow in colour and hang in loose, downwardly arching clusters from early summer to the frosts. It often self sows.

Cultivation

A well-drained, sunny site is best. It is usually treated as a half-hardy annual and planted out immediately after the last frosts.

It can grow too vigorously in the greenhouse before planting out and it can be disappointing if you *rely* on it to overwinter. In mild areas it will overwinter but will sometimes be cut back hard. However, in mild seasons it can be in flower again in spring and will then flower right through to the first bad frosts. Plants which have survived the winter should have all dead growth cut back to live shoots in spring.

Propagation

Sow in a propagator at about 65°F (17°C) in early spring, prick out into 3-in (7.5-cm) pots and then on into 5-in (12.5-cm) pots as necessary. Grow just frost free once established and pinch out the tips to keep the plants bushy. Harden off and plant out after the last frosts.

Uses in the garden

This climber grows well up a sunny trellis, on wires or trained through a stout shrub. An overwintered plant will produce a lot of growth so good support is necessary.

There are several good variegated ivies. Hedera helix 'Goldheart' has small leaves with an attractive bright yellow centre splash.

Alternatives

The true species is the most attractive but there are also three mixtures, 'Fireworks', 'Anglia Hybrids' and 'Tresco', with flowers in various reds, oranges and yellows. A lovely golden yellow and a carmine are available as separate colours.

Hedera helix
'Glacier'

Self-clinging evergreen
Hardy, to 10ft (3m)

SELF-CLINGING purplish stems carry small leaves with three to five sharp lobes. The leaves are greyish green with irregular silvery patches and usually a narrow, pale margin.

Cultivation

'Glacier' is very adaptable as to soil and situation though it dislikes waterlogged soil and will not thrive in parched sites. If the plant is to be grown up a wall or fence, fix the shoots in place with sticking plaster to encourage the aerial roots to grip. Pinching in the early stages will encourage widely spreading growth. If grown as ground cover, peg down shoots with stones to encourage spread in the right direction.

Propagation

Pegging shoots down will also encourage stems to root and these can easily be detached from the parent plant and replanted in autumn or spring.

Uses in the garden

This is a fine fence-clother for dull corners, its pale foliage adding light to otherwise dark spots. It's also a good ground cover and background to dwarf bulbs and it can also scramble through low shrubs like *Cotoneaster horizantalis*, where it looks wonderful with the red berries and autumn tints. It is good in hanging baskets for winter and spring.

Alternatives

Amongst the smaller-leaved ivies 'Goldheart', with its bright yellow central splash, is superb and the yellow 'Buttercup' is also excellent. The larger-leaved *Hedera colchica* 'Sulphur Heart' is another variety that has yellow-splashed foliage.

area required and weaker twiggy growth cut out entirely. Once established, an occasional old branch can be removed to encourage fresh growth if necessary. Side shoots that have flowered can be cut back to 3–4in (7.5–10cm).

Propagation

Cuttings 3–4in (7.5–10cm) long can be rooted in a propagator in summer or 9-in (23-cm) hardwood cuttings can be set outside in late autumn. Alternatively, shoots can be layered.

Uses in the garden

This very adaptable rose is good trained on a wall or fence, though preferably not in direct sun, or it can be grown on a pillar or pergola. It also makes a broad free-standing shrub and is occasionally grown as a hedge.

Alternatives

'New Dawn' is a semi-double, slightly more vigorous rambler that is less fragrant.

Rosa
'Madame Gregoire Staechlin'

Free-flowering rose
Deciduous scrambler,
to 20ft (6m)

A HYBRID BETWEEN the white 'Frau Karl Druschki' and the deep red 'Chateau de Clos Vougeot', this was introduced in 1927 and is a strong-growing, once-flowering climbing rose which can reach 20ft (6m) in height. The hybrid-tea-type flowers appear in early summer in prodigious quantities and are soft pink, slightly darker on the reverse of the petals. Bright hips follow in the autumn. The flowers are very strongly scented.

Cultivation

An open site and any fertile soil will suit this variety. On planting, trim back dead shoot tips and tie in new growth to wires. In following years cut back side shoots that have flowered to just 3in (7.5cm) in spring. Well-established plants should have an occasional old shoot removed low down to encourage new growth.

Propagation

Cuttings 3–4in (7.5–10cm) long can be rooted in a propagator in summer or 9-in

A thornless Bourbon rose, Rosa 'Zephirine Drouhin' is strongly scented and has attractive young foliage. It is best trained on a wall or fence, but will also make a free-standing shrub.

Rosa
'Zephirine Drouhin'

Thornless Bourbon rose
Deciduous scrambler,
hardy, to 20ft (6m)

I NTRODUCED IN 1868, this rose is rumoured to grow wild in Turkey. A thornless Bourbon rose of moderate growth with pale carmine, semi-double flowers throughout the summer and autumn, it has a strong scent and the young foliage is a rich coppery red. This is the only commonly seen thornless rose – though very occasional thorns do appear. A less vigorous thornless sport called 'Kathleen Harrop' has paler pink flowers, darker backs to the petals and translucent veins.

Cultivation

A tough, hardy variety thriving in most soils, it appreciates generous mulching or feeding in gravelly conditions. Mildew can be a big drawback. A sunny wall, shelter from wind and a dry season all exacerbate the problem. Spray regularly with a fungicide containing benomyl.

New shoots should be tied in to cover the

(23-cm) hardwood cuttings can be set outside in late autumn. Shoots can also be layered in the usual way.

Uses in the garden

This vigorous rose is good on high walls and fences of any aspect. A late-flowering clematis for a companion would provide colour later in the summer.

Alternatives

'Felicité et Perpetué' is pale ivory with a strong scent but is more vigorous and flowers a little later.

Parthenocissus henryana

Autumn-tinted Virginia creeper
Deciduous, self-clinging, to 30ft (10m)

THIS VIRGINIA creeper grows wild in Central China and was introduced to Britain by the plant hunter Augustine Henry in 1900. It is a vigorous self-clinging climber reaching over 30ft (10m) with deeply lobed foliage. The leaves are greenish bronze in colour with pink, often white, veins. In autumn the whole plant turns scarlet. There are also small, dark blue berries. This plant is unusual in that it clings to walls by means of adhesive suckers attached to tendrils, rather than short roots growing out of the stems.

Cultivation

A little shade brings out the best leaf colouring and the plant is not fussy as to soil, poor drainage being its only dislike. Early growth

Renowned for its autumn tints, the Virginia creeper (Parthenocissus henryana) is a vigorous self-clinging climber with handsome deeply lobed foliage. It does best in shade.

needs guidance to ensure the appropriate area is covered and occasional pruning in spring may be needed both to encourage business in the early stages or keep the plant in bounds later.

Propagation

New plants can be grown by layering shoots in the autumn and detaching and replanting the young plants a year later.

Uses in the garden

It is ideal for clothing shady walls; the leaf colour is not so good in full sun. However, it can be tender in the coldest areas and does not cling well to timber fences.

Alternatives

Only *P. tricuspidata* comes anywhere near it and is without the attractive leaf markings, though it is more vigorous.

Hydrangea petiolaris

Vigorous climber for cool walls
Hardy, to 50ft (15m)

IT GROWS wild in Japan, Korea and Taiwan and is sometimes supplied inadvertently in place of the similar *Schizophragma hydrangeoides*. A slow starter, but eventually strong-growing self-clinging deciduous climber, it reaches 50ft (15m) in time. The flowers are similar to those of its bushy lacecap relations, but up to 10in (25cm) across and appearing in early summer. This can be a very slow plant in the early stages and it tends not to flower until well established. The flowering period is not as long as one would like. The bare stems are an attractive winter feature. Apart from the ivies, there are few self-clinging climbers and even fewer with such showy flowers. Once the plant gets going it clings very well.

Cultivation

A well-drained, medium or light soil improved with organic matter suits it best. Shoots need support until the aerial roots begin to cling and if only one or two shoots are produced, a little pinching may be necessary. Unwanted growth can be removed after flowering.

Propagation

Layers can be made by pegging down low branches so they will root.

Uses in the garden

A showy climber for cool walls and tall fences, it can also be trained up into a tree. If used to clothe a short stump it eventually forms a low spreading bush.

Alternatives

Schizophragma integrifolium and *S. hydrangeoides* are similar but less easily obtainable and are often less successful on shady walls.

Ipomoea
'Heavenly Blue'

Long-flowering morning glory
Half-hardy, to 6ft (1.8m)

THIS STUNNING morning glory is a twining half-hardy annual reaching about 6ft (1.8m) with clusters of 2–3-in (5–7.5-cm) sky-blue trumpets similar to those of greater bindweed. The flowers only last a day but appear constantly from mid summer until into autumn.

Cultivation

A sunny spot sheltered from wind is necessary, together with a fairly fertile soil that doesn't dry out. Give some initial support to guide the twining stems to trellis, wire or a supporting shrub.

Propagation

Soak the seeds overnight then sow them individually in small pots in early spring at 70°F (20°C). Grow them on warm and harden off very carefully before planting out after the last frost.

Uses in the garden

The flowers open early and fade by afternoon so plant this climber where you can

This stunning morning glory (Ipomoea 'Heavenly Blue') is grown as a half-hardy annual in temperate climates and needs a sunny, sheltered spot to flourish.

Solanum jasminoides
'Album' is a particularly
attractive white-flowered
climber which blooms
for a long season, from
summer onwards.

see it when the flowers are open. Trellis, clematis netting, wires, other climbers and wall shrubs, and medium or large shrubs make excellent supports. The enchanting sky-blue colour of this variety looks wonderful growing through grey eucalyptus, soft pink climbing roses or, surprisingly, even the orange of *Eccremocarpus scaber* (see above).

Alternatives

There is a number of other good varieties, including 'Scarlet O'Hara' in bright red and a mixture containing purples, lavenders, pinks and blues. New from Japan is a range of varieties in chocolate, red picotee and white.

Solanum jasminoides
'Album'

White-flowered potato vine
Evergreen scrambler,
to 20ft (6m)

THIS IS THE white form of a greyish-blue-flowered species which grows wild in Paraguay and southern Brazil. It is quick-growing reaching 20ft (6m) in good locations and supporting itself by its twisting leaf stalks. The leaves give off a disagreeable smell when crushed. Pure white flowers, like those of potatoes, appear from early summer until autumn.

Cultivation

The potato vine should be planted more deeply than you would normally plant and in a sunny, sheltered spot that is reasonably well drained. As a precaution against frost injury in the coldest areas, cuttings should be taken in late summer and overwintered in a frost-free greenhouse. Its tenderness is a definite drawback but late spring planting will give it time to get established. Tie in new shoots as they grow and cut out dead wood in the spring.

Propagation

Cuttings 3–4in (7.5–10cm) long can be rooted easily in a propagator in late summer.

Uses in the garden

This is a splendid plant for a tall pergola or for covering a sunny wall or fence. It can also be trained into a tree.

Alternatives

Solanum crispum 'Glasnevin' is hardier and a most excellent plant.

Lathyrus
'Diamond Wedding'

Pure white sweet pea
Hardy sweet-scented annual, to
10ft (3m)

THE SEMI-MULTIFLORAS are characterized by exceptionally vigorous growth and very long, strong stems carrying more flowers than the average Spencer type of sweat pea. Other varieties in the group include 'Nancy Colledge' (deep pink), 'Pat Mitchell' (rose pink), 'Gypsy Rose' (deep rose) and 'Fiona' (salmon on cream). 'Diamond Wedding' is a very sweetly scented pure white type.

Cultivation

Any improved or fertile soil in a site that gets sun for at least half the day suits this variety. Dead heading is essential to prolong the flowering season.

Propagation

Sow seed in autumn or early spring, putting five seeds in a 5-in (12.5-cm) pot of loam-based seed compost, and set the pot in a cold frame. Pinch out the tops when they are about 3in (7.5cm) tall and plant the whole potful out later in spring.

Uses in the garden

It can be grown up cylinders of netting for cut flowers or garden display or through netting pinned to a fence, or will scramble through shrubs or other climbers.

Alternatives

Other good whites include 'Royal Wedding' and 'White Leamington'. In addition to the other semi-multiflora types try 'Noel Sutton' (deep blue), 'Midnight' (dark maroon) and 'North Shore' (blue and white bicolour). (See also page 88.)

Tropaeolum peregrinum

Yellow-flowered canary creeper
Hardy annual, to 12ft (3.6m)

A VIGOROUS HARDY annual scrambler that grows wild in Peru and Ecuador, the Canary Creeper supports itself by the stalks of its small lobed leaves. The frilled yellow flowers stand up singly all along the stems from mid summer to late autumn. It self seeds freely.

Cultivation

A sunny or partly shaded site in any reasonable soil suits it well. If planted in shade it will grow quickly towards the light. This plant is said to be vulnerable to attack from cabbage white caterpillars but this has not been my experience.

Propagation

Sow outside in early spring in groups of three or four below the supports. Self-sown seedlings can be moved if you find them growing in unsuitable spots.

Uses in the garden

It is at its best scrambling through other climbers and shrubs and can also be grown up trellis and wire. It looks especially good growing through purple buddleias or red climbing roses, or taking over after wisterias have finished.

Alternatives

Disregarding the rather coarse climbing nasturtiums, only the red-flowered perennial *T. speciosum* is a match for it. Unfortu-

nately this is unpredictably fussy in its requirements but seems to grow best in a leafy soil in cooler areas.

Lonicera × brownii
'Fuchsioides'

Brilliantly coloured semi-evergreen
Hardy twiner, to 10ft (3m)

THIS IS A hybrid between the evergreen, rather tender *L. sempervirens* and the tougher, small-flowered *L. hirsuta*. The hybrid is closer to the former parent and is a deciduous or semi-evergreen twining climber with rather downy leaves which are slightly bluish underneath. Its height will depend on the way in which it is pruned. The orangy-scarlet flowers are carried in clusters at the tips of the shoots in late spring and again towards the end of summer. Unlike many honeysuckles this variety is not scented and it is a great favourite with blackfly.

Cultivation

It grows best in a sheltered situation such as against a warm wall where it can either be trained up wires or allowed to grow through a stout shrub. Any reasonably fer-

Lonicera × brownii 'Fuchsioides' blooms twice, in spring and again towards the end of summer, its orangy scarlet flowers carried in clusters at the tips of the shoots.

tile soil is suitable though this variety will not thrive in poorly drained conditions. Little pruning is generally necessary although the occasional removal of an old branch low down will encourage the growth of vigorous new shoots to clothe the lower stems.

Propagation

As with many climbers, layering is the most effective method of propagation unless you want to raise large numbers.

Uses in the garden

Train it through a stout shrub, up a rustic pole and into a tree or up netting.

Alternatives

There are quite a few other good honeysuckles of which the best is certainly the coppery yellow *Lonicera × tellmaniana* which almost took the main entry, but even this has no scent. Another variety, 'Graham Thomas', is selected on page 86.

Wisteria sinensis

Vigorous scented climber
Deciduous, to 100 ft (30m)

FOUND WILD in central China, this very vigorous, twining, deciduous climber can reach 100ft (30m) when grown through a tree. It carries strings of highly scented lilac flowers up to 12in (30cm) long in late spring and sometimes again in late summer. Like all wisterias, it can be very slow to settle down and begin flowering. The variety 'Prematura' flowers quickly but the blooms are fewer and noticeably less dramatic. Seedlings vary in quality so it's wise to buy a named variety to be sure of a good plant. 'Prolific' is probably the best but seems to be unavailable at present.

Cultivation

A sunny situation and a well-drained soil are all that is required but because this plant is so vigorous, careful and thorough preparation pays off. Beware of overfeeding as this may delay flowering. Plant in spring and tie in the long wispy shoots as they grow. Pruning consists of shortening side shoots to about 6in (15cm) after flowering and then in winter cutting them back further to only two or three buds. To keep the plant small, treat all shoots in this way. Obviously

this is impractical for plants trained through trees which can simply be left to grow.

Propagation

Layering is the best method. Peg down shoots in the autumn and cut the new plants off and move them a year later.

Uses in the garden

It can be trained on fences and is splendid on pergolas or arbours where the flowers can hang down over a path. It also looks spectacular on a substantial tree.

Alternatives

The purplish-lilac flowers of the much less vigorous *W. floribunda* 'Macrobotrys' hang down to an astonishing 3–4ft (0.9–1.2m) but are less fragrant.

Wisteria sinensis is one of the most vigorous climbers. It carries strings of highly scented lilac flowers in late spring. Although it takes a while to establish itself, it will eventually make 100ft (30m) or more in the right conditions.

WALL SHRUBS

SOMETIMES I wonder why people plant hedges at all. It's always said that they make a good background for other plants but surely a fence or trellis clothed with a variety of shrubs makes a far more interesting screen. It's true that the fence and the shrubs will cost more than a hedge, but is there any more tedious job than clipping a long hedge? The appeal of a selection of wall shrubs far outweighs the dubious pleasure of a long band of green.

In large gardens, hedges may be crucial to the structure and atmosphere, but in more modest ones, where variety is so important, you should go for fences, trellis or post and wires and an interesting variety of shrubs that are happy to be trained flat against them.

I had particular criteria in mind when making this choice. There are plants which have a long period of interest, from flower, fruit or foliage, as some are evergreen. I've kept in mind pruning needs too; the simpler the pruning required, the more likely it is to actually get done. Then there's the fact that a warm, sunny wall really is an opportunity to be savoured and it pays to choose carefully and grow a fine plant that really needs those conditions.

And as with all these selections I've tried to pick plants which are not too difficult to find in nurseries or garden centres.

An autumn-flowering shrub, Hebe 'La Seduisante' needs a sunny corner to do best. Its attractive magenta-purple flower spikes appear for a long season.

Hebe
'La Seduisante'

Autumn-flowering border plant
Evergreen, to 4ft (1.2m)

THIS IS a long-established French hybrid which received an RHS Award of Merit in 1897. A vigorous, well-branched, evergreen shrub, it may eventually reach 4ft (1.2m) but can easily be kept to 2–3ft (60–90cm). The lustrous light green foliage has purple undersides when young and as the young foliage is folded together when it first emerges, the tips appear to be purple. The impressive spikes of flowers are about 4in (10cm) long in deep magenta-purple and they appear from mid summer until well into autumn.

Cultivation

A well-drained soil and a sunny site are essential to ensure that plants survive wet and cold winters happily. In very severe winters frost can cause the basal stems to split, killing the plant. Many plants will shed their seed and seedlings will come up nearby. In very bad winters which kill the parent these seedlings may well survive. However, the quality of the plants which result from these seedlings will be extremely variable, with few of real garden merit.

In rich soils plants can be trimmed back every spring and also cut back to about 6in (15cm) every two or three years. It is, however, essential to ensure that plants are fed well and not allowed to get too dry after hard pruning or they may simply die.

Propagation

Cuttings root very easily in mid and late summer.

Uses in the garden

This is a wonderful plant for late summer when many others are past their best. It is at its best in a sunny corner surrounded by other sun-lovers.

Alternatives

There is quite a range of large-flowered hybrids in a similar vein. 'Amy' has deep purple flowers and purplish foliage, 'Alicia Amherst' is bluish purple with long narrow leaves but is more tender than most and 'Simon Delaux' is rich crimson.

Choisya ternata

Sweet-scented flowers
Evergreen, to 6ft (1.8cm)

THIS SHRUB grows wild in Mexico and was introduced into the UK in 1825. A rounded evergreen, the Mexican orange blossom reaches about 6ft (1.8m) and has glossy, aromatic foliage. Clusters of sweetly scented flowers appear mainly in early summer but the sunnier the site the longer the plant will flower, sometimes still blooming at Christmas, occasionally having a few flowers in mid winter.

Cultivation

Any reasonable soil suits it and it will flower longest on a sunny wall or fence. A cool wall also suits it in most areas but the season of flowering will be much restricted and it may suffer if exposed to cold winds or from occasional frost damage in bad winters. Train the main shoots to wires and let the plant bush out from the wall. No annual pruning is usually required except the removal of the occasional frost-damaged shoot. A little careful balancing of growth may also be needed. On rich soil the removal of one third of all growth at the base in spring will encourage more vigorous shoots and improved flowering.

Propagation

Pegging down low branches with a stone will soon produce rooted shoots which can be severed and transplanted.

Uses in the garden

Its rounded habit, most noticeable on sunny walls, makes this plant a striking feature in a long border. A small-flowered clematis, such as a *C. viticella*, can look well scrambling through it. The plant is often densely clothed in evergreen foliage from the fence or wall right round to the soil and this makes it a favourite site for various nesting birds.

Choisya ternata *has the double attraction of glossy, aromatic evergreen leaves and sweetly scented white flowers.*

Alternatives

There is only one other variety, 'Sundance' with yellow foliage, but it's altogether a weaker-growing and more tender plant.

Azara microphylla

Richly scented in winter
Evergreen, to 15ft (4.6m)

THIS SHRUB grows naturally in Chile and neighbouring Argentina and was introduced in about 1861. It is a tall evergreen that can reach 15ft (4.6m) in ten years. The rounded leaves are small, dark and glossy with toothed edges. Clusters of small yellow flowers appear at any time from late winter into spring depending on the weather. These flowers have the most intoxicating vanilla fragrance. Sometimes said to be tender, this is by far the toughest of the group and although it may well be damaged in very severe winters it's very rarely killed. It can sometimes be grown in the open as a small tree, depending on the climate.

Cultivation

Any fertile soil which is neither very dry nor very wet suits this plant. It can either simply be planted against the wall and left to grow naturally or six to eight shoots can be tied in, making a fan. Little pruning is necessary though it may eventually need reducing in size.

Propagation

Cuttings 3–4in (7.5–10cm) long can be rooted in a heated propagator in late spring and summer.

Uses in the garden

Eventually a tall plant, this is best planted on a house wall near a door or gate where the winter fragrance can be appreciated. A sunny wall will encourage early flowering, but it's fairly adaptable and is only less than hardy in the coldest areas.

Alternatives

There is a pretty, smaller-growing, variegated variety, 'Variegata'. *A. lanceolata* has larger, longer leaves, is a little more tender and flowers later; it's best by the sea. *A. dentata*, *A. petiolaris* and *A. serrata* are all worth growing in milder areas.

The delicate pale yellow flowers of Jasminum nudiflorum *help to give colour to the garden in winter.*

Jasminum nudiflorum

Excellent, delicate, winter-flowerer

Very hardy, to 10ft (3m)

THIS SHRUB grows wild in south-west China and was introduced by the plant hunter Robert Fortune in 1844. It is impressively adaptable but its straggly unkempt habit is more than made up for by the reliability of its bright yellow winter flowers. Green stems scramble everywhere and carry a succession of flowers from late autumn until early spring.

Cultivation

Any reasonable, or even unreasonable, soil seems to suit this plant. Pruning is crucial both to create the best looking plant and to promote maximum flower production. The branches of young plants should be trained to wires as they grow, then the shoots that

break from them will arch down attractively. These shoots will carry the flowers in winter. After flowering all the growth that has flowered must be cut back ruthlessly to two buds. If this regime is not followed two things will happen. The whole plant will become a mass of tangled growth with the new growth shading out the old, leaving it dead and unsightly underneath. Secondly, flowers will be few and scattered.

Propagation

Lax branches will root where they touch the ground.

Uses in the garden

A fence or wall of any aspect suits this accommodating plant. Site it where it can be reached without too much trouble as the flowers are invaluable for picking for Christmas arrangements with yellow variegated shrubs and red berries. This plant is also very effective when it is planted at the top of a retaining wall and allowed to tumble over.

Alternatives

There's nothing quite like the winter jasmine unless you count its variety, 'Aureum', with leaves spattered with yellow.

Carpenteria californica

Planted by Gertrude Jekyll

Evergreen, to 6ft (1.8m)

THIS SHRUB GROWS wild in California and was introduced to Europe in about 1880 and flowered for the first time in the garden of Gertrude Jekyll at Godalming in Surrey in 1885. It is a neat evergreen, eventually reaching about 6ft

(1.8m), with glossy foliage which sets off the brilliant white flowers perfectly. These flowers are 2–3in (5–7.5cm) across, well scented and come in clusters of three to five, each with a yellow centre, mainly in early and mid summer. Older specimens develop attractive flaky bark on the lower branches.

Cultivation

It grows best in a well-drained soil that is not too rich. This shrub tends to branch well from the base and is not easy to train to wires. It's therefore best planted a little further from the wall or fence than is normal and left to grow more or less naturally. No annual pruning is necessary although the tallest shoots may become weak and should then be cut out at the base from where replacement growth springs up.

Propagation

It is more difficult to root than most shrubs, though some success may be had from striking 3–4-in (7.5–10-cm) cuttings in early summer in a heated propagator. Layering may also prove successful.

Uses in the garden

It should be planted on a sunny aspect.

Alternatives

'Ladham's Variety' is more vigorous and has larger flowers but is very difficult to find.

Fremontodendron
'California Glory'

Brilliant flowers throughout summer
Evergreen, to 15ft (4.6m)

THIS IS a hybrid between an unusual form of *Fremontodendron californicum* and *F. mexicanum*. It arose amongst a group of seedlings grown from seed of the former that was sown in 1952 in Rancho Santa Ana Botanic Garden in Orange County, California. A plant of the other parent was growing nearby. This very quick-growing evergreen shrub can reach 15ft (4.6m) or more but is easily kept to a reasonable size by pruning if necessary. The foliage is almost emerald green above and furry brown below and the big lemon yellow cups are up to 2½in (6.5cm) across. They appear in early summer and continue

in great profusion until autumn. Plants have a tendency to die suddenly when apparently thriving, but usually not before the age of about eight by which time they will have made substantial shrubs.

Cultivation

This plant does best in a rather poor but well-drained soil. It's best planted while still quite small as larger plants resent disturbance. Plants are usually single stemmed and if this stem is tied into wires the plant

Fremontodendron *'California Glory' needs a sunny wall and does best in poor but well-drained soil.*

A tough evergreen, Pyracantha 'Mohave' produces clusters of white flowers in spring followed by its chief glory – large bunches of bright orange fruits from summer till autumn.

Pyracantha
'Mohave'

Evergreen, with autumn berries
Very hardy, to 10ft (3m) or
more

THIS IS a hybrid between the rare *Pyracantha koidzumii* from Formosa and *P. coccinea* which originates from southern Europe. It is a spiny evergreen shrub of widely spreading habit and moderate vigour. Clusters of white flowers in early summer are followed by big bunches of orange-red fruits from late summer well into the autumn.

Birds are sometimes said to eat other varieties in preference to this one but I'm yet to be convinced. Many varieties of pyracantha are susceptible to fireblight, a bacterial disease which also attacks hawthorn, cotoneasters and other plants in the rose family, though not roses themselves. 'Mohave' is resistant and is also said to be resistant to the fungus disease, scab.

Cultivation

Most reasonably fertile soils, except for wet clay, are suitable and this plant also tolerates biting, icy winds and ferocious frosts especially well. Young shoots should be trained and tied in to ensure a good coverage of the wall or fence, but once set on the right course little tying will be required except on windy sites. If wayward branches need removal they should be cut back well into the plant to ensure that its natural shape is kept. If it's necessary to keep the plant growing fairly flat against the wall, the current season's growth can be cut back after flowering without reducing the same season's fruit.

will usually branch naturally and the side shoots can then be tied in as well. Little pruning is called for except the judicious removal of the tallest branches at a low branch junction when the plant starts to outgrow its space.

Propagation

Cuttings about 3–4in (7.5–10cm) long can be rooted in early spring but the success rate is likely to be low. Although plants can be raised from seed, the results will be unpredictable.

Uses in the garden

A sunny wall is the best site and a fairly light soil is preferable. A dressing of sulphate of potash in late summer is sometimes suggested to help this and other slightly tender plants to ripen their growth in time for the winter.

Alternatives

The two parents are good plants but less hardy than the hybrid. A new variety called 'Pacific Sunset' has recently appeared and has deeper yellow flowers.

Propagation

Plants grown from berries will be unpredictable but cuttings about 3–4in (7.5–10cm) long taken in summer will usually produce a few plants.

Uses in the garden

Any aspect is suitable except for a wall or fence in direct sunlight; indeed this plant thrives on cool walls. It can also be kept very tightly clipped and even trained to fit around windows and doors. Clematis and other clinging or twining climbers can be planted beneath.

Alternatives

The orange-red 'Lalandei', raised in 1874, is the most popular variety and there are also the excellent scarlet 'Watereri' and the rich yellow *Pyracantha atlantioides* 'Aurea'.

Buddleia fallowiana

Unusual butterfly bush
Deciduous, to 10ft (3m)

THIS DECIDUOUS shrub grows wild in Yunnan in China and was introduced in 1921. It can reach about 10ft (3m) but is easily kept to about 6ft (1.8m). The flowers appear from early summer to autumn and are a delicate pale lavender in colour in spikes up to 15in (38cm) long. The young foliage is grey and woolly and the leaves remain so underneath. Hardiness can be a problem in the coldest areas.

Cultivation

Any well-drained soil and sunny site is suitable. Regular mulching with compost or manure in spring or a fertilizer dressing is helpful. It can be pruned hard in spring like the more familiar buddleias and new growth is then tied in as it grows. But this tends to lead to all the flowers being produced high on the plant. Alternatively a permanent framework of branches can be tied into the wall and side shoots cut back to the lowest pair of buds each spring. Most of the new growth from the base is cut out except for one or two shoots each year which are tied in and eventually replace some of the oldest branches in the framework.

Propagation

3–4-in (7.5–10-cm) cuttings root very easily at almost any time from early spring to late summer, and those taken in spring will flower on short plants in their first summer. Young plants will happily overwinter in a cold greenhouse.

Uses in the garden

This butterfly bush covers a wide space quickly and is easily kept to a specific height, so is a fairly adaptable plant.

Alternatives

The white-flowered variety 'Alba' is probably more universally acclaimed but the lilac is a delightful shade. The hybrid between this plant and the familiar *B. davidii*, known as 'Lochinch', is much hardier and rarely requires a wall or fence. *B. crispa* is a little hardier and has smaller flower spikes but whiter foliage.

Buddleia crispa *grows quickly, like all the buddleias, producing attractive spikes of lavender flowers in summer.*

Cytisus battandieri

Pineapple-scented flowers
Evergreen, to 12ft (3.6m)

THIS SHRUB grows naturally in the Atlas mountains in Morocco and was introduced in 1922. It first flowered in a greenhouse at Kew in 1928 but was soon found to thrive outside. It is a tall, upright, evergreen or sometimes only partially evergreen shrub reaching up to 12ft (3.6m). The foliage is divided into three large leaflets covered in soft, silky white hairs. In early summer there are fat heads of brilliant yellow flowers which have a delicious pineapple scent.

Cultivation

It grows vigorously in any well-drained soil

and a sunny site but is best sheltered from strong winds, especially if left unpruned. A system of renewal pruning is normally the most successful.

Unlike most brooms, *Cytisus battandieri* regularly produces new shoots from the base which should be used to replace older growth that can be cut right out. If the lanky branches are left in, the plant tends to become top heavy.

Propagation

Cuttings can be taken in mid summer but this is a shrub easily grown from seed. The large seed should be chipped with a knife or filed with a nail file, then soaked overnight in water before sowing in a heated propagator.

Uses in the garden

It is best planted against a house wall where it can be allowed to grow freely although if grown against a fence it can still be kept to a reasonable size by renewal pruning. A sunny aspect is best.

Alternatives

There's nothing else that is quite like this impressive plant.

Clianthus puniceus

Distinctive scarlet flowers
Tender evergreen, to 5ft (1.5m)

THE LOBSTER CLAW grows wild in New Zealand and was introduced to the UK in 1831. An evergreen shrub ideally suited to wall training, it has dark green divided foliage which can be almost luxuriant when the plant is happy. The distinctive scarlet flowers are shaped like a lobster's claw (or a parrot's beak) – hence its common name – and hang in strings of up to a dozen.

Cultivation

A warm, sunny wall and a well-drained soil are essential. Even so this is not a plant for colder areas. It is tender and will be killed in the coldest winters and may be damaged in many. It also has an unfortunate tendency to die suddenly for no apparent reason. Growing tips should be pinched out occasionally to encourage bushy growth and the shoots trained into a fan shape on wires. Cut out any dead shoots in spring.

Propagation

Plants are easily raised from seed sown in a propagator in spring, so even if they are killed by frost they can easily be replaced.

Uses in the garden

The flowers need to be fairly near a path so that their shape can be appreciated. The back of a narrow border is ideal and the plant can be fan-trained on a wall behind.

Alternatives

There is a pretty white-flowered form which also comes true from seed.

Abutilon × suntense

Handsome flowers
Half-hardy, to 6–8ft
(1.8–2.4m)

THIS IS A hybrid between two wild species from Chile, *A. vitifolium* and *A. ochsenii*, which was first seen at an RHS show in 1969. The plant was raised from seed bought from Thompson and Morgan as *A. vitifolium* 'Album'. This seed originated from Highdown Garden in Sussex. It soon transpired that other hybrids had appeared from seed under the name of both parents bought from T&M, all originating at Highdown. When Chris Brickell, now Director General of the RHS, went to Highdown to investigate, he found that the plants of the two species, which used to grow side by side, had both died and self-sown seedlings of the new hybrid were flourishing in their place. This is an upright, semi-evergreen shrub reaching about 6–8ft (1.8–2.4m) in height. The large hibiscus-shaped flowers, up to 3in (7.5cm) across, appear mainly in late summer and early autumn and are a lovely clear lilac shade. The grey-green foliage is also attractive.

Cultivation

The protection of a sunny wall, together with well-drained soil, is necessary to keep this slightly tender plant happy in winter. The leading shoot should be trained to a cane tied to horizontal wires and some side branches can also be tied in. Don't try to train it absolutely flat on the wall, but allow plenty of space for it to grow out. Little pruning is usually required. However, dead heading will help prevent heavy crops of seed weakening the plant.

The only possible problem with this plant is that it can occasionally die quite suddenly after flowering when apparently in the best of health. A fertile though well-drained soil, dead-heading and regular mulching or feeding will help.

Propagation

Take 3–4-in (7.5–10-cm) cuttings in summer and root them in a heated propagator.

Uses in the garden

Its bushy habit makes this an ideal plant for the corner between south- and west-facing walls and fences, or either of those aspects. Annual climbers can be trained through it to give colour later in the year.

Alternatives

Also good is the variety 'Jermyns', slightly deeper in colour, which arose at about the same time as the plants from T&M but as the result of deliberate hybridization at Hillier's Nursery.

The two parents, especially *A. vitifolium*, are also worth growing and the white form and the free-flowering 'Veronica Tennant' are the best to look out for.

Garrya elliptica
'James Roof'

Sturdy evergreen
Hardy to 15ft (4.6m)

THIS IS a selected form of the wild species from California and Oregon and was introduced here in 1828. An evergreen shrub eventually reaching about 15ft (4.6m), it is easily restricted to manageable proportions if necessary. The foliage is deep green and rather greyish underneath. In winter the pendulous, silvery olive catkins appear. Although said to reach over 12in (30cm) in length, sometimes the catkins on my 'James Roof' reach only $8\frac{1}{2}$in (22cm) – though this is still longer than the 4–6in (10–15cm) of the ordinary variety. Garryas carry male and female flowers on separate plants and the male ones, like this one, are very much more attractive and also shed large amounts of pollen.

Cultivation

Any well-drained soil is fine and this plant also has a good tolerance of salty winds and atmospheric pollution. Although wall or

fence protection is beneficial, any aspect including a shady one suits it well. Tie in just two or three main branches to ensure stability in winds. Little or no pruning is usually needed except perhaps to restrict the size. In that case the offending branches can be removed low down in the bush in spring. It can be trained flat against the wall by trimming back when the catkins fade but tends to flower better when left to grow naturally. Branches occasionally begin to blacken and die unpredictably, though the reason for this is not known.

Abutilon × suntense *needs a sunny wall and well-drained soil to produce its large, hibiscus-shaped lilac flowers in late summer.*

Propagation

Cuttings about 4in (10cm) long can be taken in mid summer in a heated propagator and though the success rate will not be high, a few should root. Layering is also an option.

Uses in the garden

A fence or wall of any aspect will suit it, although icy winds are not appreciated.

Alternatives

'James Roof' is not easy to find in nurseries but the ordinary species, *Garrya elliptica*, is an excellent plant.

Chaenomeles
'Rowallane'

Hardy crimson-flowered
japonica
Deciduous, to 5ft (1.5m)

Raised at Rowallane garden in Northern Ireland in 1920, this is a spreading, deciduous, spiny shrub up to 5ft (1.5m) high. The large, showy flowers appear in very mild spells in winter and throughout spring in an eye-catching shade of bright crimson. Flower power can be limited and growth excessive unless an organized pruning regime is adopted.

Cultivation

This 'japonica' is very tolerant and very hardy and will succeed in all but the worst soils. Avoid over-generous feeding. Pruning greatly increases the flowering of this plant. Build up a fanlike branch structure by buying a bushy plant and training the shoots to wires. To encourage generous flower production a system similar to that used for apples is the most successful. All young non-flowering shoots are cut back to two or three buds in winter and in summer new shoots are pruned to five leaves unless they are needed to increase the area of coverage.

Propagation

3–4-in (7.5–10-cm) cuttings set in a heated propagator in summer usually root without too much difficulty.

Uses in the garden

Almost any aspect except a draughty, shady site suits this plant and its dense growth when pruned as recommended makes it an ideal support for lightweight climbers.

Alternatives

There are many other varieties of which the lovely white-flowered 'Nivalis' is almost equal favourite.

Ceanothus
'Autumnal Blue'

Californian lilac
Evergreen, to 10ft (3m)

This hybrid was raised by Burkwood and Skipwith whose nursery has long since vanished from Kingston-on-Thames in Surrey. The parentage is uncertain but includes the excellent *C. thyrsiflorus*. An evergreen, this ceanothus reaches up to 10ft (3m) but is easily kept below that height. The leaves are glossy and three-veined and the young shoots flushed with red. The deep blue flowers come in huge numbers of large spikes from mid summer until the autumn and early winter.

Cultivation

It prefers a reasonably well-drained and fertile soil but is otherwise not too fussy. Establishing a fan-shaped framework is useful in the early stages. Later, pruning is best done by cutting back towards the base of the previous year's growth in spring. Keeping the plant well clothed near the base can be difficult. This can be helped by planting a very well-branched specimen or cutting back poorly branched young plants hard to encourage plenty of low growth.

Propagation

Cuttings 3–4in (7.5–10cm) long can be rooted in a heated propagator in mid summer.

Uses in the garden

A sunny wall or fence is preferred. This variety makes an ideal host for a variety of climbing plants, in particular one of the more delicate clematis.

Alternatives

There is a number of other excellent ceanothus that make good wall shrubs. 'Gloire de Versailles' is deciduous but flowers in summer and autumn and 'Delight' is evergreen but flowers in the spring.

GROUND COVER

THE POINT of ground cover plants is quite simply that they spread out sideways, cover the soil densely and smother weeds. They also need very little attention. So while reducing the amount of work required in weeding, division and re-planting they create an attractive, if not startling, display and neatly fill the spaces around specimen plants.

This approach is sometimes an excuse for the mass planting of extremely boring plants – such as the depressingly dull *Pachysandra terminalis*, whose only virtue seems to be its ability to survive almost anything. This should not be necessary. There are many plants which will form ground cover if planted in the right way. Border phlox will suppress few weeds if you put in just one plant and then leave a gap before planting something else. If you put in three or five plants, fairly close together, even in their first year they will make a broad clump that will cover the soil and let few weeds through.

However, the plants that I've chosen as the best ground cover plants are more typical in that they are mostly spreading in habit and have a long season of interest, particularly through foliage colour. They are also easy to propagate so that once you've bought one or two plants you can quickly build up enough stocks to make a broad planting. Use them amongst specimen shrubs and perennials and other, less helpful plants to create an attractive border.

Finally, there's one very important point to remember about ground cover plants – they won't smother weeds that are already in the soil. Always clear the soil well first and then plant your ground cover and other plants, and ensure that they're kept weed free for a year or two until they are well established.

Pulmonaria saccharata
'Margery Fish'

Dense-covering foliage plant
Hardy, to 12in (30cm)

THE SPECIES is said to grow wild in woods in northern Spain; this variety was named in honour of Margery Fish who made the wonderful cottage-style garden at East Lambrook Manor in Somerset. Large oval, pointed leaves that are distinctly rough to the touch arise from a steadily spreading rootstock. In this variety the leaves are marked with large, silvery-white blotches, leaving only a few patches of dark grey-green. The flowers appear in early spring, open in pink and then turn to blue as they mature. This fine foliage plant has the added bonus of very pretty flowers.

Cultivation

Although it grows best in at least partial shade and in a fairly fertile soil, this variety will also perform reasonably well in dry shade. Mildew can be troublesome in hot dry conditions and plants may also wilt in hot sun. Giving it at least partial shade should solve both problems. It increases well and will need dividing occasionally to keep it in check.

Propagation

Clumps can be divided in spring and will yield plenty of small pieces to plant or give away. Seedlings are likely to be similar but not usually as good.

Uses in the garden

This rather special lungwort is good with purple foliage such as *Euphorbia amygdaloides* 'Rubra' or Bowles' golden grass, *Milium effusum* 'Aureum'. It is also effective in front of the variegated border phlox, especially 'Harlequin' with its pinkish tinges. Along a path, the arching pointed leaves soften the edge attractively and under deciduous shrubs of all sorts it makes a

Pulmonaria saccharata *'Margery Fish' has the bonus of elegantly marked leaves and attractive flowers, pink at first, turning blue later.*

good dense cover. Plant small pieces quite close together for the best effect.

Alternatives

There are many other good varieties including 'Argentea' with foliage that is entirely silver save for a fine dark marginal line and 'Alba' with large, pure white flowers.

Alchemilla mollis

Easy-going foliage plant
Hardy perennial, to 12in
(30cm)

FOUND GROWING wild in Asia Minor, this attractive perennial was introduced to Europe in 1874. It reaches about 12in (30cm), making a mound of sycamore-shaped, slightly hairy leaves which retain water droplets delightfully. The flowers come in rather floppy, airy sprays in mid summer and are made up of large quantities of almost lime-coloured, or pale yellow-olive-coloured flowers, making a lovely, soft green haze.

Cultivation

Lady's mantle is an amazingly tolerant plant, growing well in all but the driest shade. It will thrive in heavy or light soil and in sun or shade. Trim off the flower heads as they fade; the foliage will continue to form a pretty mound and you will also get a few more flowers. In good soil you can even cut off all the top growth after flowering and it will still grow back well. If you don't dead head, you will find that soon your whole garden is full of lady's mantle. Although it is a lovely plant, too much of it can be rather tiresome.

Propagation

If you leave a flower head on to set seed you will soon have enough self-sown seedlings to keep you going, or you can divide plants in spring.

Uses in the garden

A wonderful companion to shrub or, indeed, modern roses, it looks good either in a mixed border or in a rose bed.

Alternatives

The only plant I would like to mention here is a variety called 'Robusta' which has taller, more upright flowering shoots ideal for cutting for the house.

Acaena
'Blue Haze'

Creeping perennial
Hardy, to 8in (20cm)

ACAENAS COME originally from Australia, New Zealand and South America. Their names are rather confused as different names are used for the same plant and one name is sometimes applied to different plants. 'Blue Haze' is also known as 'Pewter' and is occasionally said to be more correctly named *A. saccaticipula*. Until the situation is clarified, it will help to read catalogue descriptions carefully and try to make sure you see plants at nurseries before you buy them.

'Blue Haze' is a creeping plant with stems that lie on the ground. The woody branches carry small rose-like leaves in an unusual smoky blue shade. In late summer there are globular, dark rusty-coloured flower heads on red stems. The whole plant reaches no more than about 8in (20cm) at most.

Lady's mantle (Alchemilla mollis) makes splendid ground cover as it self seeds readily, and it will grow well even in dry shade.

Cultivation

It grows happily in sun or wall shade but does less well when shaded from overhead by tree branches, especially if the soil is very dry and dusty. It will thrive in relatively poor soil, as long as it's not waterlogged, or heavy soil that has been improved with a little grit or organic matter. Generally, it is very tolerant. Occasional trimming may be necessary if it strays on to the grass or invades more choice plants, but otherwise it is generally trouble free.

Propagation

Seedlings occasionally turn up around the plants and often retain the colour. But pegging down shoots with a stone, as with so many ground cover plants, soon allows you to bulk up stocks for a mass planting.

Uses in the garden

It looks best at the front of the border, although its smoky haze can be attractive running through shrubs at the back. It looks wonderful with *Carex comans* 'Bronze Form' and also with low, variegated grasses.

Alternatives

There's quite a number of other varieties around. 'Copper Carpet' is a dusky, coppery shade, *A. adscendens* is larger than most with red flower heads.

Ajuga reptans 'Atropurpurea'

Purple carpeting plant
Hardy, to 6in (15cm)

THIS IS a British native plant which grows along the edges of damp woods and in other damp, shady areas. It is a low, creeping plant with long, almost evergreen foliage in rich, shining, metallic bronzed purple. In spring there are short upright spikes of blue flowers. Although it does not make a perfectly weed-free cover, it's worth planting just for its unusual colouring.

Cultivation

Full sun is best, to bring out the leaf colour in its richest tones. Although it will grow in a dryish spot, it often looks less than content, especially in summer, and a heavy or water-retentive soil suits it best. Occasional division and re-planting may be necessary when gaps start to appear or, as sometimes happens, it creeps from where you plant it to a spot a little further down the border.

Propagation

Rooted pieces can easily be detached in spring or autumn and replanted.

Uses in the garden

It is good at the front of the border where it will creep into other ground coverers and its blue spikes will appear through the foliage. It will fit itself around the boundaries of other plants, leaving no bare soil.

Alternatives

There are many other good varieties available. 'Braunherz' is a new one with purplish-bronze foliage and very tall flower spikes. 'Burgundy Glow' comes in various pinks and wine shades, 'Pink Elf' is taller and more vigorous with pink flowers and 'Variegata' is delightful; with creamy edges to the grey-green leaves, and blue flowers.

Ajuga reptans
'Atropurpurea' *is an attractive creeping plant with metallic-looking foliage and blue spring flowers.*

Stachys lanata
'Silver Carpet'

Silver carpeting plant

Hardy, to 6in (15cm)

THE CORRECT name for this species is *Stachys byzantina* but *S. lanata* is much more commonly used and *S. olympica* is sometimes seen. One famous nursery lists different varieties under all three names. The species grows wild in Iran and 'Silver Carpet' was raised by a nursery called W. Cunningham and Son of Heacham in Norfolk. Known as lamb's ears or lamb's lugs, it has large, oval leaves heavily felted with white hairs. They spread out on rather woody stems, making a lovely carpet. 'Silver Carpet' is a form which never, or very rarely, flowers and is ideal for providing ground cover.

Cultivation

Lamb's ears grows best in a well-drained but not dry soil that is reasonably fertile. Sun or a little shade will suit it well. After a wet winter it can look pretty awful as the moisture can collect on the leaves and encourage them to rot. So a tidy-up in spring is usually necessary. If any flower stems do appear they are best cut out to maintain the carpeting effect. Mildew can occasionally be a problem too.

Propagation

Clumps can be pulled apart and replanted in spring and this will usually yield plenty of spares. Alternatively, a few pieces can easily be detached from an established clump without disturbing it too much.

Uses in the garden

A good front-of-the-border plant, it looks good with the soft pink *Diascia vigilis*, although this will need keeping in bounds as it can spread a little too aggressively. It can also be used as an edging to rose beds and with dwarf campanulas.

Alternatives

There are other varieties, though here too there is some confusion over the names. 'Primrose Heron' has pale yellow leaves, 'Cotton Boll' was selected by Sheila Mac-Queen and has silvery bubbles on the flower stem but no actual flowers, and 'Sheila MacQueen' is said to have very tall flower spikes but sometimes turns out to be the normal flowering type.

Stachys lanata 'Silver Carpet' rarely flowers and makes an ideal carpeting plant in well-drained soil.

Lamium maculatum
'Beacon Silver'

Shade-loving silver-foliage plant

Hardy, to 12in (30cm)

THE SPECIES, *Lamium maculatum*, grows wild in Europe and has now been introduced to the British countryside from gardens and is sometimes

Lamium maculatum 'Beacon Silver' is a striking silver-leaved dead nettle and is particularly useful for ground cover under trees and shrubs.

found in hedgerows. This variety has been around for about ten years. It is a silver-leaved dead nettle that makes a spreading ground cover, rooting from its stems as they lay on the ground. The roughly heart-shaped leaves are entirely silver, save for a very narrow, dark line at the edge. In spring the spikes of magenta two-lipped flowers stand up from the foliage.

Cultivation

It thrives in the shade of trees, as long as the soil is not too dry, and in wall shade. In my garden it does best in a fairly well-prepared soil which seems to encourage it to remain leafy in the centre. Trimming with shears helps encourage fresh new foliage. Leaf spot, a disease that causes reddish-green spots or blotches on the leaves, is sometimes troublesome. Spraying with a fungicide containing propiconazole (e.g. Murphy Tumbleblite) is said to work, but plants in good soil are less prone to the problem.

Propagation

'Beacon Silver' roots very easily from cuttings for most of the summer so if clumps begin to look ragged it's easily replaced. It pays to cut back the dead flower spikes after flowering or after seeding if you fancy a few self-sown seedlings. These will turn up in small numbers and will usually be reasonably like their parents.

This is the pink-flowered Bergenia *variety* 'Bressingham Salmon'. *Both this form and the white-flowered* 'Bressingham White' *are valuable ground-cover plants for sun and shade.*

Uses in the garden

This is one of the few grey foliage plants that will thrive in shade and therefore is very valuable for that purpose. It makes a good spring carpet for stout bulbs like grape hyacinths, though not everyone likes the colour combination.

Alternatives

Other varieties of this species include 'White Nancy', similar but with white flowers; 'Aureum', a slow-growing variety with yellow leaves, each with a small white central stripe; 'Cannon's Gold' with a yellow leaf without a stripe; and 'Roseum' with dark green foliage with a white stripe and rose-pink flowers. There is also a new variety called 'Pink Pewter' which has white foliage and soft pink flowers.

Bergenia
'Bressingham White'
Best new bergenia
Hardy, to 12in (30cm)

INTRODUCED JUST a few years ago by Bressingham Gardens, this is a pure white bergenia with large, rather upright, rounded leathery leaves, often turning red at the edges. The flowers appear in spring in tall branched heads which usually just over-top the foliage. It is one of the most stunning of spring plants. However, if you're rigid in your dislike of these 'elephant's ears', as many people are, then I doubt whether even this handsome variety will persuade you.

Cultivation

It grows well in most reasonably fertile soils in sun or shade and will also put up with neglect and inhospitable sites. In rather gravelly but improved soil in full sun, mine has spread well and flowers profusely every year. It needs little attention apart from dead heading and a little tidying up in the autumn. It is a determined, rather than rapid, spreader.

Propagation

I find that once a plant has been growing for a few years if you mulch heavily it will root into the mulch and the fat shoots can then be detached and replanted. It doesn't need dividing at all and will be quite happy for years if just left to spread slowly.

Uses in the garden

Between deciduous shrubs, or at the front of the border, it makes a stark change from carpeting plants. It makes a neat edging to overhang on to paving.

Alternatives

'Bressingham Salmon' is an unusual colour for a bergenia, but less strong growing and less floriferous. 'Bressingham Ruby' is a new variety with lovely deep red flowers. 'Ballawley' is very large leaved and vigorous with tall spikes of intense pink flowers; in rich soil it's positively luxuriant. *B. cordifolia* 'Purpurea' has reddish-purple leaves and pink flowers.

Vinca major
'Variegata'

Variegated periwinkle
Hardy, to 9in (23cm)

THIS PLANT is also often seen labelled 'Elegantissima'. The plain green-leaved version grows naturally in mainland Europe and north Africa. This variegated version of the large-leaved periwinkle has glossy, oval foliage, each leaf boldly splashed in creamy yellow. The stems arch attractively and root where they touch the ground. In spring the young shoots carry large, starry blue flowers, though not usually in great numbers.

Cultivation

It grows well in sun or shade. Once planted, it spreads better if you place stones along or at the ends of the shoots to encourage rooting. It can be slow to start in dry, shady conditions. Once you have a good carpet you can cut down the old growth in early spring so that the flowers on the new shoots are easier to see.

Propagation

Rooted pieces can easily be detached in spring or autumn for replanting.

Uses in the garden

This colourful variegated periwinkle is good under trees or amongst summer-flowering shrubs, where it will be especially noticeable in winter when the shrubs are bare, and may even climb up into the branches a little. It also conve-

niently colours awkward spaces alongside driveways or at the base of a shed where you need to prevent weeds but where there is not really space for anything else.

Alternatives

The two other varieties of this useful species, apart from the plain green-leaved version, are 'Reticulata' and 'Surrey Marble', the latter known also as 'Maculata'. 'Reticulata' has leaf veins picked out in yellow and is rather slow growing and 'Surrey Marble' has a much more yellow central splash.

Phalaris arundinacea
'Picta'

Variegated grass
Hardy, to 4ft (1.2m)

THIS IS the variegated version of a British native plant which is common in wet places. An invasive, variegated grass, it reaches up to 4ft (1.2m) in height when in flower. The leaves are bright green and striped along their length in white. In winter the foliage remains and turns an attractive dark straw shade. In summer, fluffy beige flower spikes appear. When the plant is in flower the uppermost leaves become almost entirely green. This does not mean that the plant is reverting, but, if plain green plants do appear, remove them at once or they will swamp the clump.

Vinca major 'Variegata' has attractive yellow-splashed foliage and starry blue flowers in spring. It grows well in most situations.

Cultivation

The ribbon grass or gardeners' garters grows in almost any conditions from standing water to gravelly borders in sun or shade. Its rampageous habits are modified by the conditions in which you plant it. Set it in rich, damp soil in full sun and it will run the length of the border before you've put the trowel away. In dry shade it could almost be said to form a clump. To curb its vigour you can either let it rip and plant it amongst sturdy shrubs such as hollies, or dig it out every other year.

As its flowers fade it begins to look very tatty indeed. The answer is to cut the whole plant back to ground level. A fresh new crop of leaves will then appear but will usually stay relatively short.

Propagation

Hardly a problem with a plant that spreads with such enthusiasm. Pieces can be detached, replanted and watered in at almost any time of the year and when you lift the clump to confine it to its allotted space you will have plenty to spare.

Uses in the garden

It is best planted where it can have space to run or where it can be lifted and replanted regularly. It looks good with blue hostas or mixed with the almost equally rampant *Achillea* 'The Pearl'. I have seen it encroaching on a clump of catmint in flower and the two looked most attractive.

Alternatives

The grass it is most usually compared with is the creamier-coloured *Glyceria maxima* 'Variegata', that also has a pinkish flush to the young growth.

Symphytum
'Hidcote Blue'

*Vigorous ground-covering
plant*

Hardy, to 18in (45cm)

FOUND AT Hidcote Manor in Gloucestershire, this pretty comfrey is sometimes reckoned to be a variety of *Symphytum grandiflorum* but as it is taller, it may be *S.* × *uplandicum*. It makes a dense, aggressive, completely weed-free carpet of rough green foliage and is splendid in early summer when it throws up tubular flowers on branching 18-inch (45-cm) stems. These open red, then turn to blue, creating a delightful picture.

Cultivation

It grows well in any reasonable soil in sun or shade but is liable to invade other less aggressive plants so it needs watching carefully. If the flower heads are left on, it may well self sow freely in places where you don't want it, so by cutting the dead heads off low, you not only save yourself some tiresome weeding, but also encourage new leafy growth at the base of the plants – which helps with weed smothering.

Propagation

Divide the roots in spring or autumn.

Uses in the garden

It's especially effective in dappled shade under trees or amongst tall, stout shrubs and also makes a lovely clear haze of colour at the back of a large border.

Alternatives

'Hidcote Pink' is pink and white. *S. grandiflorum* is lower growing, has darker leaves and the flowers – rusty orange in bud, opening to cream – appear in spring.

Symphytum 'Hidcote Blue' rapidly makes a weed-free carpet in sun or shade, but because it is so vigorous, it has to be preventd from smothering less aggressive plants.

Rubus tricolor

Vigorous carpeting plant
Hardy evergreen, to 10ft (2.5m)

THIS UNUSUAL bramble grows wild in western China and was introduced in 1908. It is grown for its evergreen foliage and stem colour. The stems creep along the ground, rooting at the tips. The heart-shaped leaves are dark green with a deep shine and white underneath. What really catches the eye are the stems, lined with long, dense, gingery hairs. Its questing shoots can grow as much as 10ft (2.5m) in one season in rich soil, but usually make rather less than that.

Cultivation

It does well in dry or moist sun or shade, and is especially good for covering rough areas where little else will grow. It pays to cut back the new growth by half each spring as this will increase the density of the cover and prevent weed penetration.

Propagation

This bramble roots both at the tips and along the stems and rooted pieces can be detached and replanted. If few pieces produce roots, stones put on the shoot tips or leaf joints should help.

Uses in the garden

It is ideal for covering rough banks and large areas under trees, even those which cast a dense shade. Your can use it also as a quick weed-suppressing cover beneath shrubs.

Alternatives

There's nothing quite like it except the much smaller and restrained *R. calycinoides* which is neat enough to be recommended for the rock garden.

Geranium renardii

Valuable ground-covering
plant
Hardy, to 12–14in (30–35cm)

THIS GERANIUM was introduced from the Caucasus mountains in 1935 by Walter Ingwersen who founded Ingwersen's nursery in Sussex which specialises mainly in alpines and other small plants. Rounded clumps of soft, grey-green,

Rubus tricolor is a very vigorous, spreading ground cover with dark green heart-shaped leaves. It makes ideal cover for rough banks and will grow in quite dense shade.

lobed leaves (each deeply veined) make a dense and impenetrable cover about 12–14in (30–35cm) high. This cranesbill would be worth growing for its beautiful foliage alone but in late spring and early summer there come the very pale, slightly lilac-tinted, white flowers marked with fine purple veins. It is not a quick spreader but does form dense cover.

Cultivation

It is easy to grow in a sunny site with reasonably well-drained soil. The mass of dead growth needs clearing away the moment the first new shoots start to grow in spring.

Propagation

Although it spreads slowly it grows enough branches from its rootstock to be cut and divided up every other year. It can also be grown from seed and self-sown seedlings will usually appear.

Uses in the garden

At the front of a sunny border, it will not spread across the grass or path too much and makes the perfect foil for cool blue irises and old-fashioned roses.

Alternatives

Hardy geraniums are amongst the most popular of ground cover plants and there's a very large number of varieties available. *G. endressii* 'Wargrave Pink' flowers for a very long period with silvery-pink flowers and is discussed in more detail under Border Perennials (page 125). *G. phaeum* has dusky purple flowers with reflexed petals

In a shady border or amongst shrubs, Epimedium alpinum will cover the ground with delicate heart-shaped leaves.

like a cyclamen (there's also a lovely white form). *G. × magnificum* has big purple flowers and 'Johnson's Blue' is particularly bright blue.

Epimedium alpinum

Elegant foliage plant
Shade-loving, to 10–12in (25–30cm)

THIS GROWS wild in central Europe and has been introduced into the UK where it still survives wild in a few places. The creeping rootstock throws up wiry stems about 10–12in (25–30cm) high, carrying leaves divided into heart-shaped leaflets of soft green. The edges of the new leaves are beautifully edged in red. The open heads of flowers appear in spring.

Cultivation

This is a shade-loving plant for any reasonably fertile soil from sandy soils with extra organic matter to improved clay soils. Wall or fence shade or dappled shade from trees suit it well.

Propagation

Although they can be divided in spring or autumn they must be re-planted at once and not allowed to dry out.

Uses in the garden

Place epimediums at the front of the border so you can appreciate their flowers. They can also be planted amongst shrubs.

Alternatives

E. × versicolor 'Sulphureum' has pale yellow flowers and coppery-tinted young growth, *E. × warleyense* has orange flowers and rather spiny foliage and *E. × youngianum* 'Niveum' is pure white.

Phlox
'Oakington Blue'

Carpeting plant
Hardy, to 6in (15cm)

ALTHOUGH THIS is placed under *Phlox subulata* it is probably a hybrid and may include blood from *P. bifida* and possibly other species. This is an old variety which has been popular for many years. A flat carpet of narrow, almost mossy foliage makes a dense cover and in spring is transformed into a reflection of a summer sky as the single blue flowers completely hide the foliage. This phlox is not all that attractive in winter, when the brownish shoots may show through the sparse foliage – but spring brings a real improvement.

Cultivation

Full sun or slight shade are essential, as is a well-drained soil. Otherwise this is a very easy and tolerant plant.

Propagation

As with many creeping plants, pegged-down shoots will root or they will root from cuttings. Take short cuttings about 2–3in (5–7.5cm) long in mid summer from shoots at the base of the plant and root in a cold frame or greenhouse in a mixture of equal parts of peat and grit or perlite.

Uses in the garden

It is at its best in light soil where it will creep harmlessly on to the path and the shade of neighbouring shrubs will fix its boundaries. It will also tumble down walls and hide the more unsightly ones very effectively.

Alternatives

I selected this variety for its especially lovely colour but there are many others in various shades that are as good. 'Benita' is lavender with a darker eye, 'White Delight' is white while another old variety, 'Temiscaming', is dark pink. The varieties of *P. douglasii* grow more densely and are less vigorous.

FOLIAGE PLANTS

Foliage is crucial to a garden. Flowers come and go quickly – some too quickly to get a mention – but foliage is with us all summer and in many cases lasts all the year round.

However, it's important not to let this lead you to fill the garden with variegated and coloured-leaved plants at the expense of good old green. Green is vital as a basic ground colour and to act as a harmonizing influence and so set off both flowers and other coloured leaves. With careful thought and planning, borders made up almost entirely of yellow and golden foliage can be created but it's very difficult to make them look as good as borders with an occasional yellow-leaved plant strategically placed among the green. Silver and grey borders are a little less difficult: most flower colours associate better with silver than with yellow.

My selection takes in both shrubs and herbaceous plants, together with one of the only two conifers in the book. Many plants chosen in other sections also have attractive leaves, be they green, coloured or with autumn tints; so these are not the only foliage plants I've chosen.

Hosta
'Frances Williams'

Variegated large-leaved hosta
Hardy perennial, to 3¹/₂ft
(1.05m)

First spotted on a nursery in Connecticut by the eponymous Ms Williams, in effect it's a yellow-edged version of *Hosta sieboldiana* 'Elegans' and was first introduced as 'Yellow Edge'. It is a large-leaved hosta reaching up to 3¹/₂ft (1.05m) in height. The foliage is around 12in (30cm) across, rather crinkled and bluish-grey in colour with an edging band of creamy yellow which darkens and becomes less intense as the season progresses. In summer there are flowers in a slightly dirty white in stubby heads.

Cultivation

It grows most happily in moist half shade or dappled shade, but will reach its maximum height in full shade, though looking rather ungainly. It will also thrive in sunnier spots, as long as the soil is not too dry, and even in dry soils will produce a reasonable display, though it will be noticeably reduced in size and impact.

Propagation

Hostas are best left to form dense spreading clumps but if you're desperate for more this is what to do. In spring, when the fat buds are starting to expand, take either a spade or, better still, your best and sharpest bread knife and cut out a wedge with at least one bud from the more or less round clump:

Hosta 'Frances Williams' is one of the best and most attractive of new varieties for foliage and flower display in shady sites.

don't remove more than a quarter. Replant the wedge and fill the space in the mature plant with used potting compost.

Uses in the garden

A big clump is very striking and owing to its size, the centre of the bed or the back of a suitably broad border are the sites usually chosen. I've also seen it used at the edge where it shades out the grass. In such a place it also seems rather intimidating unless seen from a distance. It looks good with tall blue campanulas.

Alternatives

H. sieboldiana 'Elegans' is a good alternative, without the yellow margin. For a plant with a creamy margin to a strong green, rather than bluish, leaf you can hardly do better than 'Shade Fanfare', certainly a close rival to 'Frances Williams' for the top spot.

Berberis thunbergii
'Atropurpurea'

Purple foliage, with autumn tints

Hardy shrub, to 8ft (2.4m)

THE ORIGINAL species grows wild in Japan where it was discovered by the plant hunter, Thunberg, in 1794. It didn't reach the UK until late in the 19th century. The purple-leaved version was first seen in a nursery at Orléans in France in 1913. It is a spiny, deciduous shrub of neat growth, reaching a maximum height of about 8ft (2.4m), but generally rather less. The foliage is purplish, sometimes quite deep in colour, sometimes paler but often darkening as the season advances. Autumn colour is fiery red. There are also yellow flowers lining the branches in spring and red fruits in the autumn.

Although originally propagated by nurseries from cuttings, these days seed is more common. This can result in plants of slightly varying shades of purple so it's not a plant to buy by mail order. It is best to go to a nursery or garden centre and choose one whose colour you like.

Cultivation

This purple barberry seems happy in most situations that are not excessively damp but is usually at its best in a sunny position. It can also be grown as a hedge that can be cut back in spring, while specimen plants can be cut back, hard if necessary, at the same time. Otherwise little attention, save some tidying, is usually required.

Uses in the garden

Like all dark-leaved plants, it must be used sparingly to avoid a deadening effect. Personally I find hedges of this plant rather dour. Single plants which are allowed to grow to their full size are probably the most effective when climbers such as clematis – try the creamy *Clematis viticella* 'Alba Luxurians' or the rosy 'Abundance' – can be trained through them. Associated with white flowers or with foliage in silver, yellow or with bluish tones, its purple leaves look most effective.

Berberis thunbergii 'Atropurpurea' – the purple-leaved variety – is seen here contrasting well with the grey foliage of helianthemums.

Betula pendula *'Golden Cloud'* makes an excellent quick-growing specimen tree for a small garden. In addition to the yellow foliage, it has an attractive white bark.

Alternatives

A number of other purple-leaved varieties are now available, many with distinct growth habits. 'Atropurpurea Nana' is a dwarf version while 'Bagatelle' is even smaller, making a rounded hummock only 12in (30cm) high. 'Dart's Red Lady' has a semi-prostrate habit. 'Helmond Pillar' is stiff and upright in growth and 'Rose Glow' has young shoots flecked with silvery pink.

Artemisia
'Powis Castle'

Silver- leaved wormwood
Hardy shrub, to 18in (45cm)

THIS IS A hybrid of uncertain origin that arose at the National Trust garden at Powis Castle. *Artemisia arborescens* and *A. absinthum* are sometimes assumed to be the parents. It is a low, spreading shrub with finely fingered foliage in the palest grey. Quick growing, it can reach 3ft (90cm) across and half as high in one season, but this is usually because it's planted in soil which is too rich. It's smaller and more compact in suitable soil. It produces no flowers at all, so the foliage is always shown off well.

Cultivation

This wormwood is best in full sun in a well-drained soil that is not too rich. (Rich soil leads to excessive growth than can be damaged in winter by frost or the weight of snow.) A mulching of gravel shows off the foliage to best advantage and also makes a very effective weed-smothering ground cover. This is one of the hardiest of the shrubby artemesias. In winter, the weight of snow, or heavy rain, can break the side branches at the point where they join the main stem but the plant usually breaks well from low down and the broken branches can be cut right out. You must also trim off any damaged growth in spring.

Propagation

Cuttings root throughout the growing season if set in a well-drained compost in a heated propagator.

Uses in the garden

A wonderful foil for most flowering plants requiring similar conditions, such as the

soft blue twiner *Codonopsis clematidea*, this artemesia is also deliciously delicate in its own right. It is an essential constituent of the silver border.

Alternatives

'Faith Raven' is almost identical though perhaps a little smaller. *Artemisia arborescens* is similar but less hardy. *A. schmidtiana* is altogether more dwarf and more fussy as to drainage but is exceptionally silky.

Betula
'Golden Cloud'

Golden-leaved birch
Hardy tree, to 20ft (6m)

THIS TREE WAS developed in Holland and introduced quite recently. A white-stemmed birch, it reaches about 20ft (6m) and has yellow foliage all summer. The foliage is a darker reddish yellow when it unfurls but soon develops its distinctive bright yellow colour, deepening as the season progresses.

Cultivation

Plant in any reasonable soil in partial shade. Although the colour is better in full sun, the foliage may scorch unless shaded. It can be grown as a tree or as bushy shrub. If grown as a tree, little pruning will be necessary. However, if grown as a bushy shrub, it should be cut back hard to about 2ft (60cm) every spring.

Propagation

This birch is usually propagated by grafting, which is difficult for the home gardener.

Uses in the garden

As a quick-growing specimen tree its colour makes it a splendid focal point for a small garden, but beware of using too much other yellow foliage. As a shrub it is very elegant and is good with deep green hostas.

Alternatives

The only comparable yellow-leaved tree is *Robinia pseudacacia* 'Frisia' which has brilliant lime-yellow foliage.

Thuja occidentalis
'Rheingold'

Good small garden conifer
Hardy evergreen, to 4ft (1.2m)

THE WILD species grows in eastern North America and a huge range of varieties have arisen over the years. 'Rheingold' has been grown since at least the turn of the century but its actual origin is uncertain. It is sometimes confused with a very similar variety called 'Ellwangeriana Aurea'. But if you ask for 'Rheingold' you will get the plant I recommend. A neat, slow growing, more or less conical plant, it eventually reaches about 4ft (1.2m) in height. In summer the foliage is a slightly golden yellow, although the leaves on the inside of the plant remain a yellowish green. In winter the foliage takes on a rich, burnished, coppery yellow shade. The new growth in spring has a slightly pinkish tinge.

Cultivation

The colours are best if it is planted in sunny sites and it seems to thrive in both well-drained and quite moist soils. Protect it from the overhanging of other plants, especially when small, or shoots may be killed leading to an uneven shape. It can be trimmed but as growth is slow this is usually only necessary after a calamity.

Propagation

This conifer is not easy to root, but cuttings can be rooted in pots in a cold frame in late summer.

Uses in the garden

It is splendid with heathers and other small conifers but 'Rheingold' is also one of the few conifers that fit fairly well into a mixed border with perennials and other shrubs. Bergenias, small blue hostas, any flowers in coppery, orange or red tones, yellow linarias and many more go with it very well.

Alternatives

'Sunkist' is similar, but the same shade of yellow all the season.

A neat slow-growing conifer, Thuja occidentalis *'Rheingold' eventually reaches about 4ft (1.2m) in height.*

Helictotrichon sempervirens is an attractive clump-forming grass with elegant arching flower spikes in spring.

Heliototrichon sempervirens

Handsome specimen grass
Hardy, to 2ft (60cm)

THIS GRASS, found growing wild in Central Europe, is a slowly increasing, clump-forming variety, making a 2-ft (60-cm) high stiff mound of narrow, erect leaves in an especially fine, blue grey shade, that radiate from a central crown. The leaves are slightly rolled, fairly rigid and sharply pointed. In late spring elegant arching flower spikes appear and self-sown seedlings are likely to pop up in the following season. It is also sometimes listed as *Avena candida* or *A. sempervirens*.

Cultivation

The colour is best and it thrives most whole-heartedly in full sun on a fairly well-drained, but nevertheless fertile soil. On heavy clay the colour is poor and sections of the clump tend to die out if conditions are too wet. On my well-drained soil this happened recently, probably because I've forked in too much humus.

Uses in the garden

This lovely grass looks splendid in isolation in gravel and I have it with the blue-flowered *Eryngium variifolium*, creating an altogether delightful show. Other eryngiums would also be good and I've seen it bursting out of a mat of *Lamium maculatum* 'Beacon Silver' very effectively.

Alternatives

On a much smaller scale, *Festuca glauca* and the variety 'Silver Sea', which has a better colour, are both good. For a taller blue grass the recently introduced *Agropyron pubiflorum* is quickly taking my favours. It is more upright in growth and its broader foliage creates a stronger impact though it's floppier and less stylish. For a real rampager in bluish grey go for *Elymus arenarius*. It is used to bind sand dunes and will whistle the length of the border in no time if given anything approaching fertile soil.

Hakonechloa macra
'Albo-aurea'

Front-of-border plant

Hardy grass, to 12in (30cm)

IT SEEMS probable that plants known as 'Variegata' and 'Aureola' are actually exactly the same as 'Albo-aurea'. This species has also been known as *Phragmites minor*. It is the variegated version of a wild species which grows naturally in Japan with narrow leaves reaching about 12in (30cm) in height. The leaves arch forward towards the light, laying over one another, creating an effect like water streaming over a ledge. At the back of the clump the newer shoots stand up more vertically. The leaves themselves are striped in green and yellow with an occasional bronze tint. It spreads slowly and steadily but is never invasive.

Cultivation

It grows well in fertile soil that doesn't dry out and should be planted in no more than partial shade for the best colour.

Propagation

Clumps are best left to expand slowly but they can be split and replanted in spring.

Uses in the garden

An ideal front-of-the-border plant, it makes a neat yet fluffy edge and will not quickly flop on to the grass causing a bare patch. It looks good with small-leaved hostas.

Alternatives

Molinia caerulea 'Variegata', the creamy striped version of the British purple moor grass, grows in a similar way but the variegation is paler. It, too, is a splendid plant.

Hakonechloa macra 'Albo-aurea' is a variegated form of a Japanese native grass and makes an excellent front-of-the-border plant.

Elaeagnus pungens
'Maculata'

Variegated evergreen shrub
Hardy, to 12 ft (3.6m)

THE WILD species grows in Japan but the origin of 'Maculata' is not known although it was shown at the Royal Horticultural Show in 1891. It makes a tall, fairly vigorous evergreen shrub, sometimes reaching 12ft (3.6m) or occasionally more. The leaves are large, oval and splashed with an irregular central blotch of rich butter yellow. The mark is variable in size and there are often less intense yellow shades where it borders the green. It's especially dramatic in winter when its brightening effect on what might otherwise be a dull garden has to be seen to be believed. The new growth is also attractive, being covered in greyish brown scales. There are also small fragrant flowers in autumn. This variety has a tendency to produce plain green shoots and as these are more vigorous than variegated shoots they can smother the variegated growth and take over the whole plant. I've seen a plant 10ft (3.5m) high with only one small variegated shoot remaining. So it's important to prune out any plain green shoots as soon as they're seen.

Cultivation

It grows happily in a variety of soils in sun or shade although it's not happy on shallow chalk. Growth can be slow for the first year or two but speeds up later. Little pruning is normally required, except to improve the shape. If the plant gets too big it will respond well to hard pruning in spring. Any green shoots should be cut out.

Propagation

Low shoots will root into the soil if pegged down in summer and these can be separated and replanted the following spring.

Uses in the garden

This shrub can be positioned to provide a bright winter focal point with taller perennials in front to reduce the impact during the summer months. It looks excellent with purple flowers such as *Clematis* 'Niobe' or *C. viticella* 'Royal Velours' trained through it, or *Geranium phaeum* planted in front. For an almost garish foliage association, plant with the berberis mentioned earlier or a regularly pruned purple smoke bush, *Cotinus coggygria* 'Royal Purple'.

Alternatives

A slightly softer coloured variety is 'Variegata', with a creamy margin but I prefer *E.* × *ebbingei* 'Limelight' that is a little less blatant in its display but is very strong growing from the start. I have one on a cool fence which has reached 8ft (2.4m) in four years and is still going strong.

Euonymus fortunei
'Emerald 'n' Gold'

Spreading variegated evergreen
Hardy shrub, to 18in (45cm)

TO BE ABSOLUTELY correct this and other varieties should come under *E. fortunei* var. *radicans* which hails from Japan, but the name is usually shortened for convenience, especially as there has been some confusion over these names. This variety is a relatively recent introduction, and is a splendidly coloured small shrub, whose name more or less sums up its attractions. It makes a low, spreading plant reaching 18in (45cm) in height at the most, with bright, gold-edged, emerald green leaves. In winter the leaves develop purplish pink tints.

Cultivation

It is happy in most soils and situations but not at its best in hot dry sites. It prefers shade which is not bone dry. Little or no pruning is necessary.

Propagation

Shoots layer themselves into the soil under the plants and this can be encouraged by using a stone or two to hold them down.

Uses in the garden

A splendid ground-covering plant, it makes a slightly uneven carpet that fits itself round other shrubs conveniently and will peep out here and there.

Alternatives

There's quite a range of varieties with slightly different habits and distinctly varying leaf colours. 'Silver Queen' is more upright with a white margin to the leaf, 'Variegatus' has a white margin and a greyish centre, often with a pink tinge, and will climb any wall or tree it happens to meet.

Fuchsia magellanica
'Versicolor'

*Invaluable shrub for sun or
semi-shade*

Hardy, to 6ft (1.8m)

THE NATURAL species grows wild along streamsides in Chile and Argentina in company with, of all things, *Berberis darwinii*. This variety is a hardy fuchsia with narrow pointed leaves. The expanding shoots are a rich red, which pale slightly as they grow until eventually only the tips remain pink while the unfolding leaves turn a soft greyish green. Growth is arching and later in the summer small red flowers hang from the branches. In winter the branch structure is less than elegant with stout upright shoots and wiry side shoots. This is one of the hardiest fuchsias and although it may be cut to the ground in bad winters it will usually shoot again very strongly from the base.

Cultivation

It is happiest on heavier soils and appreciates moisture, though it does well in a more gravelly soil out of full sun. This fuchsia also thrives with a shady aspect, though its foliage colour is best in a sunny place. Young plants should be planted after the first frost but will withstand the winter once established. Cut it back to ground level each year when it starts to grow in spring. After a mild winter very little of the top growth is killed but it's still a good plan to cut the plant back very hard to retain its attractive arching habit.

Propagation

Cuttings taken in summer root easily, even without a propagator and plants can also be dug up and split in spring.

Uses in the garden

It brings a light airiness to semi-shaded areas, though it will not thrive not under trees, and makes a splendid permanent foundation planting for an annual change of summer plants such as the upright *Lobelia vallida*, a pale blue, bedding lobelia that will scramble through the lower branches; the dark orange cigar flower, *Cuphea ignea*; the soft blue *Salvia patens* 'Cambridge Blue'; and *Nicotiana* 'Domino White' or 'Lime Green'.

Fuchsia magellanica 'Versicolor', one of the hardiest fuchsias, is an excellent foliage plant for semi-shade.

The yellow-blotched leaves of the evergreen Elaeagnus pungens 'Maculata' look dramatic in winter, and the plant also offers the bonus of small fragrant flowers in autumn.

Alternatives

There's nothing quite like it really but another hardy fuchsia for foliage effect is 'Variegata' with its neat, regular creamy edge to the dark green leaf.

Convolvulus cneorum

Silver-leaved evergreen
Half-hardy shrub, to 3ft
(90cm)

IT GROWS WILD in Southern Europe from Italy to Greece and is a small, rather rounded, evergreen shrub reaching no more than 3ft (90cm) in height with narrow leaves covered with white silky hairs. Small clusters of white, bindweed-like flowers appear at the shoot tips in summer. As this plant becomes more popular it's increasingly seen in garden centres grown in containers in a peat compost. In winter this compost holds too much water creating a soggy area around the roots and the plant may well die even though the surrounding soil is well drained. So check the compost before you buy, or better still buy from a specialist nursery.

Cultivation

A well-drained, sunny site, preferably in a raised bed or at the foot of a sunny wall, suits it best. This shelter is essential in cold areas as *C. cneorum* is not hardy. It's not fussy about soil but good drainage is vital. Tidying up after the winter is often necessary but otherwise little pruning is usually needed. Occasionally one branch may grow especially long and should be cut out.

The silvery leaves of the evergreen Convolvulus cneorum *are as attractive as the white, bindweed-like flowers. It needs a sunny site and some shelter in cold areas.*

Propagation

Cuttings 3–4in (7.5–10cm) long taken in summer usually root fairly easily in a heated propagator.

Uses in the garden

This is an essential ingredient of a Mediterranean or silver foliage border and a good host to smaller climbers.

Alternatives

There's nothing quite like this superb plant.

Weigela florida
'Variegata'

Spring specimen plant
Hardy shrub, to 6ft (1.8m)

THE SPECIES grows wild in Japan, Korea and China. The origin of this variegated form is uncertain. It is a compact deciduous shrub, less vigorous than the more familiar green-leaved varieties and will eventually reach about 6ft (1.8m). The leaves are a slightly pale green with a creamy white margin, both shades darkening as the season progresses. The flowers, in late spring and early summer, are pink and associate perfectly with the pale foliage.

Cultivation

It's happy in full sun and any reasonably fertile soil, sandy or heavy. No pruning is usually necessary although a little tidying may occasionally be necessary. Occasional green shoots may appear and these should be cut out at once.

Uses in the garden

It makes a wonderful spring specimen and is another candidate for supporting a small-flowered clematis to flower later in the year.

Alternatives

There are at least three other coloured-leaved forms but none comes anywhere close in effect. 'Looymansii Aurea' has yellow foliage all summer and pink flowers, 'Rubigold' is a yellow-leaved sport of 'Bristol Ruby', and there's the dark-purple-leaved 'Foliis Purpureis'. For a variegated equivalent look out for *Cornus alba* 'Elegantissima' which doesn't have such showy flowers, but does have bright red winter stems.

BULBS

Selecting bulbs – that is bulbs in the broadest sense – must be one of the most difficult choices when planting a garden. The problem is deciding exactly which varieties to go for. I once visited a breeder in Holland who grew over 2,000 different types of daffodils. Not only that, but he was busy breeding even more.

Not all bulbs will thrive in a mixed border or naturalized in grass. Some will be best for showing and may need a little cossetting to thrive and produce really good flowers. Others will be better as cut flowers and be suited to the particular way bulbs are grown for this trade, or they may force well for early cut flowers but have no other use. The number that are suitable for growing in the garden from year to year is not as great as it seems – but taking just daffodils as an example, there are still hundreds that you could grow. So I hope my guidance will help.

You can grow bulbs in a number of ways. My favourite method for many bulbs is simply to plant them amongst perennials and shrubs as another way of adding colour to a particular area. They then have a good background of foliage or flowers and some ground cover to prevent splashing and to set them off when seen from above. By choosing the flower colours carefully, you can create some very pretty combinations.

When I was in Holland I noticed some gardeners had planted bulbs, especially tulips, in neat clumps with gaps in between. This is certainly a good way of showing off the qualities of the individual varieties, but I'd prefer *some* greenery in between. Another approach was to fill a whole bed with different bulbs – no gaps, simply stunning sheets of colour. Grape hyacinths are often used to link the flowing drifts of different colours.

Most of us like bulbs that can be left in the ground from year to year and which will increase – planting them for their spring colour and then taking them out is very time-consuming, but it needn't be wasteful as heeling them in and feeding them will ensure that most will be fit for another few years.

Finally, the one thing that bulbs appreciate more than anything is feeding. Whether or not they're left in all the year round, a few liquid feeds after flowering will bulk them up well for the following year.

Ornithogalum nutans

Good under-shrub bulb

Hardy, to 12in (30cm)

This plant grows wild in woods across Europe and into Turkey and is also sometimes seen apparently growing wild here in Britain, but this is the result of its being introduced. In spring it produces flowers on stems up to 12in (30cm) in height, with up to about two dozen flowers in a spike. Each flower is slightly pendulous, of a shimmering silvery white, greyish green on the outside, with the tips of the flowers rolling back. The leaves die away as the flowers are at their best.

Cultivation

It grows best in light shade and a soil that doesn't dry out, where it will increase well both by multiplication of the bulbs and by self seeding.

Uses in the garden

It happily settles in around the margins of shrubs in mixed borders and also thrives when naturalized in grass.

Alternatives

O. umbellatum carries its flowers in a flat head rather than a spike and is a regular in cottage gardens. *O. narbonense* is often seen in catalogues and has longer spikes of smaller flowers.

Crocosmia
'Lucifer'

A tall, elegant montbretia

Hardy, to 4–5ft (1.2–1.5m)

This and a number of other splendid hybrids were raised by Alan Bloom at Bressingham Gardens by crossing a number of different crocosmias including

C. paniculata, C. masonorum and *C.* 'Jacka-napes'. The resulting plants come in a variety of red, orange and yellow shades and all are worth growing. 'Lucifer' produces steadily increasing corms that throw up fresh green, rather narrow, iris-like leaves above which the flowers appear from mid summer onwards. These are brilliant scarlet and are held in long, arching spikes with the individual flowers turned upwards. It reaches 4–5ft (1.2–1.5m) in height. This is an excellent cut flower if treated correctly. In particular it's important to keep the flowers away from ripening fruit and vegetables and dying flowers. These give off ethylene gas to which crocosmias are especially sensitive.

Cultivation

It thrives in a sunny place in most soils. Mine spreads well in improved, gravelly conditions. The dry foliage and flower stems must be cut down to the ground each year in early spring.

Uses in the garden

This 'montbretia' is good in either a mixed border or a more traditional herbaceous border and might also be vigorous enough to naturalize in grass. The rather stiff, upright, sword-like foliage gives strong vertical lines. The flowers associate well with hot oranges and bright yellows; I'd like to see it grown against a purple hazel. *Achillea* 'Gold Plate' might also be a good companion, its lacy foliage and flat yellow flower heads contrasting well but not too brashly.

Alternatives

The other varieties in the series are all worth growing and include 'Emberglow', which is burnt orange, and 'Spitfire', which is a little paler and has a yellow throat. The new, slightly peachy yellow 'Jenny Bloom' is lovely. 'Solfatare' is an older and rather shorter variety with dusky bronze leaves. Unfortunately it's a little tender.

Oxalis adenophylla

Raised-bed plant

Hardy, to 2in (5cm)

THIS DELIGHTFUL plant grows wild in southern Chile and Argentina. Greyish, rue-coloured foliage makes a neat, rounded hummock not more than a

Crocosmia 'Lucifer' is one of the best modern montbretias – its brilliant scarlet flowers and sword-like foliage make a striking addition to any border.

couple of inches (5cm) high. The flowers, which appear in mid or late spring, are a pale lilac pink with dark veins and open in the sun, nestling on top of the foliage.

Cultivation

Although it demands a well-drained soil and full sun, it doesn't object to a certain amount of humus as well. Given these conditions it will surely thrive. Sometimes this plant is sold as dry tubers but these do not always establish well. It's better bought as a growing plant in a pot but it's crucial to water it well after planting or the roots may not grow out from the root ball.

Uses in the garden

As a neat clump at the front of a raised bed this plant is unsurpassable.

Alternatives

This is the easiest to grow, others are more tricky or are weeds. Try also *O. laciniata* with wavy, blue-grey, star-shaped leaves and lilac flowers with dark purple veins.

Cyclamen hederifolium

*Naturalizing cyclamen for
semi-shade*

Hardy, to 6–8in (15–20cm)

GROWING WILD over much of southern Europe from eastern Turkey to the Pyrenees, this is a small, autumn-flowering cyclamen with pink flowers which are darker and slightly streaked at the mouth of the reflexed petals. The flowers appear in late summer and early autumn and are carried on stems up to 8in (20cm) long. The foliage may appear at the same time or rather later. The leaves vary greatly in their shape and patterning, sometimes being long and narrow but usually more or less ivy-shaped. The best forms have a very attractive grey patterning. In recent years corms of this and other species have been dug up from the wild, dried off and imported. This has led to a dramatic reduction in the wild populations and the trade is now controlled. However, these dry corms very rarely grow so it pays to buy smaller, growing plants from specialist nurseries which will usually have raised them from seed.

Cyclamen hederifolium *will spread and naturalize in semi-shade and are ideal plants for lightly wooded areas or to clothe bare soil around the base of shrubs.*

Cultivation

The easiest of the hardy cyclamen, it will grow in sun or partial shade but thrives best in light or dappled shade. It prefers a soil which is neither excessively heavy nor light, but by forking in leaf mould almost any soil can be made suitable. An annual mulch of fine leaf mould is also a great help.

Uses in the garden

It is ideal in the wilder areas under dappled shade where it should self sow contentedly. The foliage of even average forms is attractive and it naturalizes well under trees and even in sparse grass.

Alternatives

There are a number of other species available and the easiest of these to grow outside are the late-winter-flowering *C. coum*, the spring-flowering *C. repandum* and the summer-flowering *C. purpurescens*. By planting all four, flowers can be had for most of the year.

Lilium regale

*Powerfully scented,
opulent lily*

Hardy, to 6ft (1.8m)

INTRODUCED FROM a single valley in western China by the plant hunter E. H. Wilson as recently as the 1920s, this lily has large, self-indulgent, white flowers that flare to show off the yellow throat and the dusty orange pollen. There is purple staining on the outside and these large trumpets give off a powerful scent. Weak plants may carry just one flower, vigorous and contented plants many more – up to 30 have been counted. The stems can be 6ft (1.8m) in height with a dense covering of foliage. It produces large quantities of seed which will quickly grow to produce flowering-size bulbs, so that a dramatic display can be achieved fairly economically. Vita Sackville-West raised many hundreds this way when making the garden at Sissinghurst.

Cultivation

This lily is stem rooting so needs deep planting in any reasonably fertile soil that is not too heavily shaded. It grows well in full sun or a shady position that is not overhung. It is occasionally damaged by spring frosts.

Spray regularly as a precaution against aphids which transmit virus. An insecticide containing pirimicarb (e.g. ICI Rapid) gives the quickest results. They don't usually need staking but do need protection from slugs as they come through in spring.

Uses in the garden

Lilies are best planted in clumps, and segregated from other lilies by blocks of shrubs or other barriers to help prevent aphids carrying virus from one plant to another. It's in large groups that they look their most striking, so plant at least ten bulbs together. They look good overtopping shorter plants such as *Salvia* 'Lubecca'.

Alternatives

There is a number of other trumpet lilies available. The florists' lily, *L. longiflorum*, is a little tender for most gardens. Various hybrids are available including 'Royal Gold' with bright golden-yellow flowers, 'Green Dragon' with white flowers, flushed on the outside with green and 'Black Dragon' with white flowers which are deep purple on the outside. The 'Olympic Hybrids' come in white, cream, yellow, orange or pink, sometimes with a contrasting colour on the outside of the petals.

Galanthus nivalis

The harbinger of spring
Hardy, to 10in (25cm)

THIS SNOWDROP grows wild in woodlands all over Europe. It's not certain whether the plants seen in British woods are actually native or have been planted. A description of this familiar, but very variable plant is hardly necessary except to say that it's distinguished from many other snowdrops by the meeting, edge-to-edge, of the leaf margins (others overlap or are reflexed), the pale streak down the centre of each leaf and the green marks at the tip of the inner petals. Many of the dry bulbs often seen for sale in garden centres have been collected from the wild in the same way as cyclamen. While it's true to say that they are more likely to settle down after planting, they are best bought 'in the green'. This means they are lifted and transplanted or sold just after flowering while the foliage is still healthy. Most mail order suppliers sell snowdrops in this way.

Cultivation

Easy to grow in cooler situations in full or partial shade, snowdrops thrive even in sun if the soil is not too dry. They flourish in heavy soils but even the sandiest will grow them well if some humus is added. It is a good idea to divide the clumps occasionally, otherwise they eventually get very dense and foliage predominates.

Uses in the garden

Snowdrops thrive and look very attractive in many situations – under trees, along hedges, in rough grass, around shrubs – indeed almost anywhere that is reasonably moist while they are growing, and not too parched in summer.

Alternatives

There are many varieties available. The double form, 'Flore Pleno', is often thought to be better for naturalizing as the flowers are more substantial and last longer so are more effective from a distance. 'Atkinsii' is a good robust, larger-flowered form.

Snowdrops (Galanthus nivalis) *herald the arrival of spring. There are many varieties available. 'Flore Pleno' (above) is an attractive double form which naturalizes well.*

Galtonia candicans

The handsome summer hyacinth
Hardy, to 3–4ft (90cm–1.2m)

The summer hyacinth (Galtonia candicans) grows particularly well on acid soils and often produces self-sown seedlings.

THIS SUMMER-FLOWERING plant grows wild in southern Africa, particularly Orange Free State, Natal and Lesotho. It reaches 3–4ft (90cm–1.2m) and has white, bell-shaped flowers in open spires, each carrying up to 30 blooms.

Cultivation

The summer hyacinth grows well on any light soils but especially on acid soils where it can build up well. It is hardy in all but the coldest areas, where the bulbs should be lifted and stored in a frost-free place for the winter. In many gardens, clumps may steadily reduce in vigour and size and eventually fade away. This is due to a debilitating virus disease. Fortunately this plant produces large quantities of seed, even when infected, and the seed does not carry the virus. Self-sown seedlings may turn up, or the seed can be sown in pots and grown on, when bulbs will reach flowering size quickly.

Uses in the garden

It is ideal in clumps in mixed borders, amongst shrubs or in herbaceous borders, giving a distinctive appearance to the summer garden. It often self sows itself attractively about the border.

Alternatives

There are two other species available, both with greenish flowers. *G. princeps* is similar to *G. candicans*, though rather smaller and with flowers in cream with a green tint, while *G. viridiflora* is pale green.

Crocus chrysanthus

Late-winter flowerer
Hardy, to 6in (15cm)

THE WILD yellow *Crocus chrysanthus* grows naturally in south-east Europe and the first varieties were selected at van Tubergen's nursery in Holland. Later the great plantsman E. A. Bowles continued the work and introduced many of those listed below. Crosses were also made with *C. biflorus. C. chrysanthus* is slightly smaller than the familiar Dutch crocus and with far more charm. The flowers come in an astonishing range of shades and bicolours, and many are striped, flushed or feathered on the outside of the petals. The colours range from the pure yellow of the wild species to white, creams, bronzes and browns, blues, grey-blues, lilacs and deep purples. They start to flower in late winter, occasionally earlier, and open best in the early spring sunshine. In cold, dull weather the flowers may not open.

Cultivation

Give them a sunny and well-drained site, though not parched soil of any type. They look best planted 2in (5cm) apart and in clumps of at least ten. A liquid feed after flowering helps them increase well. They also make good plants for pots in the cold greenhouse, in which case they should be re-potted every year in loam-based potting compost. Add extra grit if you find yourself with a particularly heavy sample.

Uses in the garden

They look well at the front of sunny borders and in raised beds amongst alpines. Low, ground-covering plants like cotulas or acaenas can be planted over them to reduce splash and to occupy the space after the bulbs have died down. If grown in pots in the cold greenhouse – and no heat at all is necessary – they can be brought indoors in bud and the flowers will open well in the warmth. As the flowers fade, return them to the greenhouse or a cold frame.

Alternatives

I am suggesting the whole group of varieties though my favourite is probably 'Blue Bird'. The flowers are rounded and mainly white, with a slightly dusky violet-blue on the outside of the three outer petals. Others to try are 'Blue Pearl' (soft blue), 'Cream Beauty' (creamy yellow), 'E. A. Bowles' (pale yellow, brownish grey outside), 'Lady-killer' (white with dark purple outside), 'Skyline' (soft blue with violet veins), 'Snowbunting' (white with a yellow centre and purplish brown feathering on the outside), and 'Zwanenberg Bronze' (gold with brown outside).

Muscari
'Blue Spike'

Adaptable, easy spring bulb
Hardy, to 10in (25cm)

THIS IS A form of *M. armeniacum* which grows wild in Greece, Yugoslavia and through Turkey. It produces dense, rather chunky spikes of small, double, rich blue flowers on floppy foliage in mid and late spring. Bulbs sold under this name are not always the true variety, some with single flowers. This affects the display a little and many self-sown seedlings appear.

Cultivation

This bulb is easy to grow in almost any situation from a mixed border to dappled shade. It spreads well and puts up with the poor conditions cheerfully.

Uses in the garden

It makes an attractive edging to other spring plantings and in Holland I've seen it used to link plantings of daffodils, tulips and other bulbs in contrasting colours.

Alternatives

The straight species is widely available but has less impact. If you prefer a white grape hyacinth go for *M. botryoides* 'Alba'.

Tulipa
'West Point'

Stylish, lily-flowered tulip
to 20in (50cm)

THIS IS AN old and well-established lily-flowered variety that flowers in late spring. The brilliant yellow flowers are broad at the base, then narrowing, and flared at the top on about 20-in (50-cm) stems.

Cultivation

As tulips are usually removed after flowering, they can be planted in almost any soil that is not too wet and any site that is not too dark. Lift after flowering and heel in a light,

One of the easiest bulbs to grow, Muscari also makes an attractive edging to other spring bulbs.

sandy soil and feed well with liquid feed. When the foliage has died down, lift and select the largest bulbs to keep for the following year. Few of the more traditional types can be left in the garden permanently and even if lifted, they usually fade away.

Uses in the garden

'West Point' is wonderful in bedding schemes with orange or deep blood-red wallflowers or forget-me-nots.

Alternatives

'Queen of the Night' is almost black and flowers in late spring, 'Orange Bouquet' has up to six flowers per stem and also flowers in late spring. 'General de Wet' is a soft orange and flowers earlier, as does the shorter 'Red Riding Hood' with its black-centred, scarlet flowers.

Narcissus
'Geranium'

Best traditional narcissus
Hardy, to 12in (30cm)

AN OLD AND familiar variety, this sweetly scented traditional 'narcissus' has up to five flowers on each strong stem, starting in late spring. Each flower is pure white with a small, deep orange flared cup. It's a robust variety which increases extremely quickly and is very reasonably priced.

Narcissus 'February Gold' is one of the earliest flowering daffodils. A sheltered spot will help to ensure early flowering, and the flowers often bloom earlier the second year after planting.

Cultivation

Like all daffodils it appreciates early planting, dead heading and liquid feeding. It grows well in pots.

Uses in the garden

In borders it will spread well and it can also be naturalized successfully in grass or dappled shade amongst trees.

Alternatives

'Scarlet Gem' is a yellow-flowered version with a dark orange cup. 'Cheerfulness' is a double-flowered white with three flowers per stem. It has a primrose-yellow sport called 'Yellow Cheerfulness'. The very fragrant 'Actaea' has just one large pure white flower per stem with a pretty red edge.

Narcissus
'February Gold'

Elegant, early-flowering
daffodil
Hardy, to 12–14in (30–38cm)

THIS DAFFODIL is a hybrid involving the dainty *N. cyclamineous*, with dramatically reflexed petals. This is still a reliable early-flowering variety. Its long trumpet emerges from flared petals, and the individual flowers are very attractive and appear on stems about 12–14in (30–38cm) high.

Cultivation

It does well in borders that do not dry out too much in sun or shade. Plant in clumps or drifts and, after flowering, feed well with a liquid feed. Little or no special attention is required. It is also good in pots.

Uses in the garden

In early borders it looks splendid with *Pulmonaria rubra* or orange polyanthus, and is best placed against evergreen foliage to show off the flowers. For flowers in late winter, a sheltered spot which gets plenty of sun is best. 'February Gold' also naturalizes in grass.

Alternatives

'February Silver' is ivory white with a pale yellow trumpet but is less robust. 'Peeping Tom' has a longer trumpet and slightly more reflexed petals, and flowers later.

SCENTED PLANTS

EVERYONE CAN say whether a rose is red or yellow but describing scent is a much more subjective exercise. First of all, around 10 per cent of people have no sense of smell at all so if I say that a columbine smells of mangoes or an arum lily smells of rotten meat it won't mean a thing to them.

Some people also have 'blind spots' relating to one particular plant. For example, I can't smell border phlox at all but other people enthuse about their fragrance. Fragrance is also more difficult to remember, so describing the smells from memory is less precise.

However, for anybody with a reasonable sense of smell, scent in the garden is a major priority. When you consider the number of packets of night-scented stocks that are sold – and no-one would buy them for their *looks* – it is obvious that people do buy plants purely for their perfume.

The fact that we disagree as to what exactly a plant smells of, or indeed whether it smells at all, means that I might choose plants that would never be on your list, but your family and friends might disagree with you too.

Buddleia davidii
'Royal Red'
Deciduous shrub
Hardy, to 8ft (2.4m)

ALTHOUGH *Buddleia davidii* was discovered in China in 1869, the main introduction to Europe came from seed collected in the early 1900s. The origin of 'Royal Red' is uncertain but it was awarded an Award of Merit by the Royal Horticultural Society in 1950 and an Award of Garden Merit in 1969. It is a vigorous deciduous shrub with long, dark green leaves that are silvery beneath, and it can reach 8ft (2.4m) in height. The branches have an attractive arching habit. The flower spikes appear at the ends of the branches from mid summer onwards in a rich reddish-purple shade and the flower spikes of this particular variety are amongst the longest produced by any buddleia. The scent is sweet and powerful. All buddleias produce so much nectar that they are a great favourite with butterflies.

Long flower spikes in rich reddish-purple distinguish 'Royal Red' from the more common forms of Buddleia davidii. *The sweet-scented flowers are a great draw for butterflies, as with all the buddleias.*

Cultivation

Full sun and a fertile soil will produce the best plants and a mulch every spring after pruning will help foster strong growth. It also pays to remove the dead flowers as they fade to encourage the side shoots to produce flowers later. If they are not dead-headed, the flowers can look tatty and brown.

You should also prune hard in spring as the buds start into growth by cutting back to within two buds of the older growth. Well-grown plants will grow 6–8ft (1.8–2.4m) during the season after this pruning.

Propagation

Cuttings taken of side shoots after flowering root easily. They can be overwintered in 3-in (7.5-cm) pots and will flower in the following year after planting out.

Uses in the garden

This is excellent as a specimen plant at the back of the mixed border with a white summer-flowering clematis or yellow canary creeper growing through it. The arching branches of this variety will bring the flowers closer to the nose.

Alternatives

Other good varieties include 'White Bouquet' which is said to have an especially strong scent, 'Black Knight' in very dark purple and 'Empire Blue' in pale lilac blue with an orange eye.

Hesperis matrionalis
'Flore Pleno'

Short-lived perennial
Hardy, 3–4ft (90cm–1.2m)

A SHORT-LIVED perennial plant that reaches about 3–4ft (90cm–1.2m) in height with tall open spikes of double lilac flowers in early summer.

The double white form known by the common names of sweet rocket, dame's violet and, strangely, close sciences, has been known since the end of the 16th century but was rare for many years. By the end of the 17th century it was widespread and the double purple appeared about this time. However, it was soon noticed that the latter was increasingly difficult to propagate and by 1884 the double purple had virtually vanished and the double white was selling for 1s 2d a plant. Most plants in gardens and on sale have yellow rings on the foliage; these are virus symptoms which are transmitted when the plants are propagated. The sweet and delicious scent is at its most powerful in the evening.

Until recently this plant was virtually impossible to obtain and this would normally disqualify it from inclusion. It's just so exquisite that I couldn't resist it. Fortunately it is now being propagated in the laboratory by tissue culture and is becoming more widely available. The single-flowered, seed-raised strains are the only ones generally available. Although they don't flower for as long and the flowers are less appealing, the scent is just as magical.

Cultivation

It grows best in a rich, moist limey soil in sun or partial shade but even given ideal conditions it's difficult to grow well, partly because of the virus infection. Propagation from short lengths of the flowering stem every couple of years is necessary.

Uses in the garden

A choice specimen plant, its look, scent and rarity mean that it should be placed where it can be cared for and treasured.

Alternatives

The seed strains belong here. In fact only a mixture seems to be available and this includes purple, lilac and white. They self sow happily in a wide variety of conditions.

Philadelphus
'Belle Etoile'

Deciduous shrub
Hardy, to 5ft (1.5m)

Philadelphus *'Belle Etoile' with its sweetly scented, starry white flowers in early summer also offers good autumn leaf colours.*

THIS MEDIUM-SIZED mock orange is a rather twiggy, deciduous shrub reaching about 5ft (1.5m) in height. The oval leaves develop good yellow colour in the autumn. The pure white flowers are about 1½in (4cm) across, each with a purplish blotch at the base, and appear in early summer. Their fragrance is delightful.

One of a number of good varieties raised by the French firm of Lemoine, 'Belle Etoile' received an Award of Merit from the Royal Horticultural Society in 1930.

Cultivation

This tough and accommodating plant thrives on most soils, acid or limey. It's at its best in full sun though will tolerate some shade. After allowing three or four years for the plant to establish well, remove one third of the flowering shoots at ground level immediately after flowering each year.

Hamamelis mollis 'Pallida' is one of the best witch hazels to grow, with its exquisite scent. Site it where you can savour the fragrance.

sery. It received the Award of Merit in 1932. It is a large spreading shrub with broad foliage that turns a lovely yellow in the autumn. The flowers appear throughout winter, sometimes stretching into early spring, and are shaped rather like spiders – the petals are long and narrow and curl and twist out from the maroon eye of the flower. In this variety the flowers are a soft, sulphurous yellow and the scent is sweet and persistent, wafting for long distances around the winter garden and filling a house with fragrance if cut. Of course if you have only one plant, it will soon have no growth left at all if you cut it. So, if your garden is a large one and you have a vegetable garden or relatively unused corner where a plant or two can be set, keep them for cutting at Christmas. Even then, don't be too hard on them.

Cultivation

A neutral or acid soil is best; limey conditions lead to sickly-looking foliage and poor growth. It grows best in full sun or half shade. Plant it where the winter sun can play on the flowers. Regular mulching is useful. No pruning is generally required.

Propagation

Most plants of this witch hazel are grafted and, as this is a tricky technique for the home gardener, new plants must be bought. However, they are expensive.

Uses in the garden

It is best in a relatively uncrowded position where it can be underplanted with spring bulbs such as aconites, snowdrops or even bluebells. The autumn colour should not be obscured by other plants set around it and the flowers must be fairly close to paths or areas you are likely to pass in winter.

Alternatives

Other good witch hazels are *H. × intermedia* 'Jelena' in coppery orange and the redder 'Ruby Glow' and 'Diane'.

Propagation

Shoots with roots can sometimes be detached at ground level or hardwood cuttings about 9in (23cm) long can be taken in late autumn and set outside in a sheltered, shady spot where they should be ready to move the following spring.

Uses in the garden

A substantial plant, it makes its presence felt in the border. Do not plant it too far from the path or the scent will strike you only when the wind is in the right direction. Between flowering and autumn colour the effect can be rather sombre so train some canary creeper or other summer-flowering climber through its branches.

Alternatives

For a taller variety with larger flowers look out for 'Virginal'. If you need a much more compact variety, try the dainty double-flowered 'Manteau d'Hermine'.

Hamamelis mollis
'Pallida'

Deciduous shrub

Hardy, to 20ft (6m)

THE WILD SPECIES grows naturally in China and was first introduced to Britain in 1879. 'Pallida' was raised at the Royal Horticultural Society garden at Wisley from seed sent from a neglected Dutch nur-

Lilium candidum

Cottage garden bulb

Hardy, to 3–5ft (90cm–1.5m)

THE MADONNA lily grows wild in Greece and the eastern Mediterranean region. It is an archetypal cottage-garden lily whose pure colour and exquisite scent should be a feature of all but the most formal gardens. It reaches 3–5ft (90cm–1.5m) in height and the outward-facing, pure white flowers appear for some weeks in early summer. After flowering the plants produce a small rosette of leaves at ground level.

Cultivation

This lily is an avid lime lover and will thrive best in a reasonably well-drained but fairly heavy soil in full sun. It hates waterlogging. The best clumps are often seen in old cottage gardens, where they have not been lifted for many years and the bulbs have become crowded and may even be sitting on the soil surface. It may be simply that the lack of disturbance suits them or it may be that because it is often the only lily grown in such gardens, the chances of virus infection are remote.

Like all lilies, the Madonna lily is prone to virus infection and this species seems more liable to attack than most. Weak growth, distorted and discoloured foliage and pale streaks in the foliage are the most common signs and you shouldn't obtain bulbs from clumps showing these symptoms. Seedlings should be virus-free and can be protected from infection by regular spraying against the greenfly that spread the disease.

The Madonna lily has only a short period of dormancy after flowering and this is the best time at which to plant. Bulbs on sale in garden centres are often dry and shrivelled, so try and beg some from a neighbour at the right time or raise your own seedlings. This is also one of the few lilies that insist on being planted right at the surface of the soil, with the tip of the bulb level with the soil surface. It goes against the grain to do this but it really is vital.

Propagation

Clumps can be lifted and bulbs replanted after flowering, or seed can be collected from your own plants and sown immediately in pots in a cold frame. They will germinate the following spring and should flower within three years.

Uses in the garden

Grow with a cottagey mixture of plants, particularly delphiniums, which flower at about the same time. Remember that after flowering there will be nothing at all to see so plant a floppy perennial such as a herbaceous clematis behind to fall forward and cover the spot.

Alternatives

Probably the easiest of the other white-flowered scented lilies to grow is the larger-flowered regal lily, *Lilium regale*. This is particularly valuable as it can be raised quickly from seed sown in a propagator in spring to flower the following year.

Rosa
'Fragrant Cloud'

Deciduous shrub
Hardy, to 3ft 6in (1.05m)

RAISED IN Germany and introduced in 1963, this is a sturdy hybrid tea rose reaching about 3ft 6in (1.05m) in height with an upright but branching habit and a dark, lustrous foliage. The flowers themselves are bright red at first but become purplish as they age. They can be very large – up to 5–6in (12.5–15cm) across.

The Madonna lily (Lilium candidum) is a regal plant with handsome pure white flowers with a delightful scent. It looks good planted in a border with delphiniums.

The strength of the scent is indicated by the fact that for many years this variety has topped the popularity poll for scented roses amongst members of the Royal National Rose Society (RNRS).

Cultivation

The standard, rather generous rose treatment will suit it very nicely – planting in full sun, a rich, fertile soil, regular mulching, and feeding with a rose fertilizer. Cut it back by half in autumn to prevent wind rock, and then prune hard in spring as the buds start to swell.

Having started off as a rose that was resistant to mildew and black spot, 'Fragrant Cloud' is now becoming more susceptible.

Propagation

All bought plants are budded on to special rootstocks, which is difficult for the home gardener. Hardwood cuttings about 9in (23cm) long can be rooted outside in a sheltered place in late autumn.

Uses in the garden

Some people say that the colour of its fading flowers can make it hard to integrate into a carefully colour-planned planting, but it's certainly sturdy enough to take the competition of a mixed border. It also looks well in a mixed rose bed, in a group or in a bed of its own.

Alternatives

The next three varieties in the RNRS poll for scented varieties were 'Wendy Cussons' – a deep pink hybrid tea, 'Margaret Merrill' – a dark-leaved, white-flowered floribunda and 'Alec's Red', a crimson hybrid tea.

Lonicera periclymenum
'Graham Thomas'

Deciduous honeysuckle
Hardy, to 15ft (4.5m)

THIS IS a vigorous, deciduous variety of our native climbing honeysuckle, reaching about 15ft (4.5m) in height. The cream flowers, which appear from early summer until autumn, differ from our native woodlander in three ways: there are more of them, the petals are a little broader so they look more substantial and the fragrance is more powerful.

Cultivation

This honeysuckle does best in a soil that

Lonicera periclymenum *'Graham Thomas' is a vigorous honeysuckle which can be grown on a shady wall or through a small tree or tall shrub.*

does not dry out and in dappled or partial shade – take a hint from its natural habits. Like so many honeysuckles, this variety can be plagued by blackfly. An insecticide containing pirimicarb (e.g. ICI Rapid) will deal with them in minutes.

To prune, thin out some of the older growth as the flowers fade, taking care not to damage the vigorous new shoots.

Propagation

Layering is again the best method of propagation, as it is with so many climbers. Simply peg down a shoot with a stone during the summer and it will root. It can be detached and planted the following spring.

Uses in the garden

It will happily scramble up a tree trunk clothed in netting or wire to provide support. A shady wall suits it too or it can ramble up a trellis or through a small tree.

Alternatives

More restrained in growth are 'Belgica', the so-called 'Early Dutch' with reddish flowers aging to yellow and 'Serotina', the 'Late Dutch' with similar flowers that appear a fortnight later. There is some debate as to whether or not these two varieties are actually distinct.

Nicotiana affinis

Evening-scented perennial
Half-hardy, to 4–5ft
(1.2–1.5m)

THE TOBACCO PLANT grows wild in South America. Its correct name is probably *Nicotiana alata* var. *grandiflora*, under which it is sometimes listed. This tall plant is a half-hardy perennial reaching 4–5ft (1.2–1.5m) in height and is always grown as a half-hardy annual. The leaves are broad, fresh green in colour but rather sticky and the large pure white flowers have a long tube and a five-pointed, flat, slightly floppy face. The flowers close during the day and open in the evening when the scent is released.

Cultivation

Plant out 18–24in (45–60cm) apart in late spring; it will usually be flowering a month afterwards. It is good in sun or half shade and will grow in most soils.

Propagation

Sow the seed in early spring in a heated propagator, prick out into 3-in (7.5-cm) pots and grow on fairly cool until planting time in late spring.

Uses in the garden

The scent is so heavy and is carried such long distances in the still evening air that there's no necessity to plant immediately alongside a path or surrounding a patio. If planting in containers, use large ones as these tall tobacco plants make a substantial amount of root growth.

Alternatives

N. sylvestris is another large, white-flowered species but the flowers are much more tubular in shape and hang from elegant, denser heads. There are a number of coloured strains. The 'Sensation Hybrids' come in a range of colours and the scented flowers stay open all day – but the scent doesn't quite match that of *N. affinis*. 'Domino' is a very dwarf variety that has virtually no scent.

The tobacco plant (Nicotiana affinis) gives off a heady scent in the evening when the flowers open. Plant them in drifts for the best scented effect.

One of the oldest of all sweet peas, Lathyrus 'Painted Lady' can be grown successfully on a netted fence or over a mature shrub.

Lathyrus
'Painted Lady'

Old-fashioned sweet pea
Hardy, to 6–8ft (1.8–2.4m)

Possibly from Ceylon originally, this is one of the oldest of all sweet peas, growing to about 6–8ft (1.8–2.4m) and clinging by tendrils. Although the bi-coloured red and white flowers, which appear from early summer onwards, are smaller than those of modern varieties, they are very pretty and produced in vast numbers. And of course the scent is like no other.

Cultivation

Grow in a well-prepared soil in a sunny site. If the soil is reasonably fertile and does not dry out 'Painted Lady' will be happy.

Propagation

Sow five seeds in a 5-in (12.5-cm) pot of peat-based compost in autumn and stand in a cold frame. Germination will take place in a few weeks and the seedlings will grow slowly through the winter. Once they've reached about 3in (7.5cm) in height, pinch out the tops to encourage bushiness. Plant out in early spring. Alternatively, seed can be sown in late winter in the same way and planted out about two months later.

Uses in the garden

A wigwam of canes, a tube of wire netting, trellis, plastic netting stretched on a fence or a mature shrub will provide suitable support. For cutting, sweet peas are best grown up plastic netting set up in an open position.

Alternatives

Many of the larger-flowered, more modern sweet peas are very sweetly scented and for scent I would recommend 'Andrew Unwin' – lavender blue; 'Diamond Wedding' – white (see page 40); 'Cyril Fletcher' – pink; 'Old Times' – cream flushed with blue; and 'The Doctor' – mauve. Collections of fragrant varieties are available from most seed companies.

Dianthus
'Mrs Sinkins'

Old-fashioned cottage pink
Hardy, to 12in (30cm)

This rather untidy garden pink has the usual narrow, grey-blue foliage (though not as blue as some). It's at its best in early summer when it flowers gloriously, though it's not restricted to that season. The flowers are pure white and they, too, are rather untidy.

The calyx (the group of overlapping leafy structures that surround the flower in bud and remain enclosing the base of the flower after it opens) splits when the flower opens and so the petals burst through the side adding to the untidy appearance of the flower. This characteristic disqualifies 'Mrs Sinkins' on the showbench but in the garden does little more than make the flowers look scrappy. The scent is very powerful and is generally agreed to be the strongest of all garden pinks.

Cultivation

This tolerant plant will thrive in a sunny site in almost any conditions from sand to clay as long as the soil is not waterlogged or parched. I would not recommend it for acid soils. Naturally, a fertile soil suits it best. It pays to replace old plants with youngsters every few years.

Propagation

Plants can be layered by the time honoured 'stone-on-a-stem' method.

Uses in the garden

It is traditionally used as an edging to a cottage front path, a vegetable garden or to beds of roses or other plants. 'Mrs Sinkins' also looks good in a group at the front of the mixed border and I've also seen it used as a carpet beneath roses.

Alternatives

'White Ladies' is said to be a better plant, with white flowers of purer colour and better form, bluer foliage and as good a scent as 'Mrs Sinkins'. Unfortunately it is less easy to find in garden centres.

Heliotrope
'Chatsworth'

Summer-bedding perennial
Half-hardy, to 18in (45cm)

NAMED HELIOTROPES were popular in the late 19th century and are mainly the result of crossing two South American species, *H. peruvianum* and *H. corymbosum*. This variety presumably arose at the house which has given it its name. It is a half-hardy perennial that is treated as a summer bedder with an open, rather spreading habit. It reaches about 18in (45cm) in height and as much across. The leaves are oval, deeply patterned with veins and rough to the touch. The flowers, whose spikes uncurl like forget-me-nots, are purple – dark at the edges and fading towards the centre with a yellowish green eye. The scent is of vanilla. Though the plant is not flamboyant, the scent is reason enough to grow it.

Cultivation

Plant out after the last frost in a sunny spot in fertile soil or in a container. 'Chatsworth' can be trained as a standard but you need plenty of greenhouse space so that you can overwinter large plants. In the coldest parts of the country, it's best when grown as a conservatory plant.

Propagation

As the plants are frost tender you'll need to take cuttings in late summer or early autumn and overwinter them in a frost-free greenhouse or conservatory.

Uses in the garden

'Chatsworth' is excellent in containers with the small grey leaves of *Plecostachys serpyllifolia* (formerly known as *Helichrysum microphyllum*). It can also be planted towards the front of the border to straggle through neighbouring plants like greyish grasses or yellow antirrhinums such as 'Coronette Yellow'.

Alternatives

Very few of these old cutting-raised varieties are now available and this is the easiest to find. If you come across any others, try them. Seed-raised strains are also available. 'Marine' is altogether dwarfer and more bushy with darker, slightly metallic foliage but virtually no scent. 'Mini-Marine' is dwarfer and has foliage that is almost bronze in colours.

Viburnum carlesii
'Aurora'

Deciduous shrub
Hardy, to 6ft (1.8m)

A VARIETY selected and introduced by the Slieve Donard nursery in Northern Ireland, 'Aurora' gained an Award of Garden Merit in 1969. It is a medium-sized deciduous shrub – even venerable specimens of this viburnum reach

The vanilla-scented Heliotrope 'Chatsworth' is best planted at the front of a border or to complement grey-leaved plants.

The reddish purple flowers of Daphne mezereum stud the branches in late winter and early spring and are delightfully scented.

little more than 6ft (1.8m) in height in normal circumstances. The leaves are a very attractive greyish green with a slightly felted underside and good autumn colour. The flowers are soft pink in colour, opening from red buds, and appear in large rounded clusters in spring. The scent is so pervasive that even when only the first one or two individual flowers are open, you can't miss it.

Cultivation

A tolerant plant, it is probably happiest in a little shade but thrives in my garden on a sunny fence and also grows well in half shade. Any soil that is not on the extremes of wet or drought will suit it.

Little pruning is usually needed though a little shaping may sometimes be necessary. Growth is not fast so cutting for the house should be done with circumspection.

Propagation

Many plants in garden centres are grafted but this variety should also root from cuttings taken in early summer and then rooted in a propagator.

Uses in the garden

Place 'Aurora' at the back of medium-sized borders or use it as a focal point towards the middle of larger ones. Once established and growing it can also be used as a host for climbers of moderate growth such as *Lathyrus tingitanus*.

Alternatives

'Aurora' has two sisters – 'Charis', which is especially vigorous in growth, and 'Diana' which is more compact. The varieties of the partially evergreen *Viburnum* × *burkwoodii* (of which *V. carlesii* is one parent), such as 'Anne Russell', are also worth growing.

Daphne mezereum

Deciduous shrub

Hardy, to 3ft (90cm)

ONCE GROWING wild in woods on limestone soils, this plant is now quite rare in its natural habitat. A deciduous shrub of upright growth, it eventually reaches about 3ft (90cm) in height. In late winter and early spring the branches are studded with reddish purple flowers which are very sweetly scented. These are followed later in the season by poisonous yellow berries which eventually ripen and turn red.

Cultivation

A shrub which is happy in a limey soil, it also prefers a soil which is fertile and does not dry out – though it dislikes waterlogging. It's best in light shade though will also do well in full sun as long as the soil is not too dry, in which case the set of fruits can be very poor. No pruning is usually required.

Propagation

Self-sown seedlings often appear under and around established plants and these can be moved to new homes while they are still young. Mature plants sometimes produce low branches suitable for layering.

Uses in the garden

It is good on a corner near a path where the scent can be savoured, or on a rock garden.

Alternatives

There is also an attractive white form, 'Album', which is worth growing.

ANNUALS & BEDDING PLANTS

For many years, although millions of bedding plants have been bought from garden centres to brighten the summer garden, there hasn't been the surge of enthusiasm for these plants that there has been for, say, alpines. However, things are changing as many gardeners are beginning to appreciate the huge range of annuals and bedding plants available. More varieties are now available in separate colours, some of the best of the old-fashioned, cutting-raised, summer bedders are re-appearing in garden centres and the development of genuinely winter-flowering pansies has revived an interest in winter and spring bedding plants.

Annuals and bedding plants have plenty of good things going for them. They're colourful – indeed many are dazzlingly brilliant – and the colour range is astonishing. Most are tolerant and easy to raise and there's a wide variety to choose from for every situation. As they're adaptable, you can plant up large beds for a stunning display or simply pop a few plants in the gaps between perennial plants. You can change your display twice a year, keeping the plants you like and the schemes that work, and abandoning the others.

In my selection I've chosen eight plants for summer and six for spring and have suggested others. I haven't included bulbs in the spring selection although they make ideal partners for many biennials and spring bedders. Sadly, some excellent plants and some old favourites – geraniums and antirrhinums – have also had to be left out as there's only room in this chapter for a limited selection.

Taygetes
'Solar Sulphur'

Easy annual

Hardy, to 12in (30cm)

Marigolds thrive in sunshine even in poor soil. 'Solar Sulphur' is an aptly named double-flowered variety which looks best planted in tubs and window boxes.

A MARIGOLD of rounded habit, it reaches about 12in (30cm) in height and has neat, fully double sulphur-yellow flowers that cover the plants. 'Sulphur' is one of a series of varieties with the 'Solar' prefix, some of the others having crested flowers; all are in shades of yellow and orange. They are very weather resistant and flower soon after sowing and then right through the summer until the frosts. 'Solar Sulphur' is an Afro-French hybrid. It produces no seed so doesn't need dead-heading and also flowers more prolifically than other varieties. Occasionally, large, very leafy plants turn up amongst the seedlings and these grow two or three times as big as the others and produce no flowers. They can be recognized by their extra vigour and lack of flower before planting out so they should be obvious and can easily be discarded.

Cultivation

Any site in the sun will suit them and they're very tolerant of unfriendly soil. Their eventual size is governed by the richness and moisture content of the soil and in very rich soil they may become rather leafy.

Propagation

The seed is large and easily sown and, because they flower so quickly, never sow before early spring. Occasionally, the first flower will not be typical but after that the display will really blaze.

Uses in the garden

They are rather too stunning to go in a mixed border where other plants may look

dull in comparison but 'Solar Sulphur' is splendid in bedding schemes in tubs and window boxes and around patios.

Alternatives

The others in the 'Solar' series are good. There's also a series of single-flowered varieties which are rather more spreading in habit – they have names like 'Nell Gwynn' and 'Suzie Wong' and I'd also recommend a dark-mahogany-flowered one called 'Red Seven Star'.

Begonia
'Lucia'

Summer-flowering annual
Tender, to 9in (23cm)

A NEAT, rounded fibrous-rooted begonia, it reaches no more than 9in (23cm) high, even in shade. 'Lucia' is a mixture in which the plants have foliage in both green and deep bronze and the flowers come in red, white and a great variety of pink shades. Altogether there should be over a dozen different types.

Cultivation

Any reasonably fertile soil that's not too dry suits them. Although they prefer a sunny site, they will do better in the shade than most bedding plants, especially if planted in borders shaded by a wall or fence rather than under a tree.

Propagation

Sow seed early, in late winter, making sure to sow thinly and hardly covering the seed. Cover with glass or clingfilm at 70°F (21°C) and keep the seed moist but not sodden. Prick out as soon as you can handle the seedlings and keep them at about 60°F (15°C) if possible, before hardening off and planting out after the last frost. The seed is very fine and difficult to sow and the tiny seedlings need careful looking after, but ready-germinated seedlings are available from some seed companies.

Uses in the garden

A small bed densely planted with this mixture can be delightful and they also make good edging or window-box plants.

Alternatives

'Devon Gems', 'New Generation' and 'Fantasy Mixture' contain the same colours but in a different blend. 'Organdy' is an older variety which is slightly taller with a good range of colours while 'Party Fun' is taller still at about 12in (30cm). There are a number of separate colours available including 'Coco Bright Scarlet' with bronze foliage and scarlet flowers; for hanging baskets and window boxes, try 'Pink Avalanche'.

Mimulus
'Malibu'

Summer-flowering perennial
Hardy, to 8in (20cm)

D EVELOPED BY Floranova, the British based plant breeder, 'Malibu' is the newest and most dwarf of their mimulus varieties. It is a creeping perennial, often known as monkey flower, almost always grown as an annual, with dark green foliage spreading out into a mat about 8in (20cm) high. The flared, mainly plain-faced flowers start to appear in late spring and continue right through the summer. The flowers come in creamy white, yellow, orange, scarlet and deep red and can appear in as little as seven weeks from the first seed sowing.

Cultivation

They are best grown in a fairly rich and water-retentive soil as if the plants dry out

Growing rapidly from seed, Mimulus 'Malibu' needs plenty of moisture to thrive. Because they are such quick-growing plants, they make ideal border fillers.

93

Chrysanthemum *'Court Jesters'* *are excellent border plants, grown in a big group, and will do well in any reasonably fertile soil in a sunny position.*

they will collapse and die. They will thrive in sun or shade if they have enough water.

Propagation

This can be difficult because the seed is so tiny. Sow in a peat-based seed compost and cover the seeds very lightly. Keep them moist though not sodden. Prick them out into pots as they grow too quickly for trays.

Uses in the garden

These new hybrids are good in shade (provided it is not dry) and at the front of the border. They are ideal for filling unexpected gaps in beds and borders quickly.

Alternatives

'Calypso' is rather taller and comes in a mixture of colours, all with spotted flowers. The startling 'Viva', at around 15in (38cm), is the tallest and is bright yellow with a uniform pattern of deep red blotching.

Chrysanthemum
'Polar Star'

Summer-flowering annual
Hardy, to 3ft (90cm)

THIS EASY-TO-GROW hardy annual will reach about 3ft (90cm) in height with a branching habit if given the space to spread out. The single, daisy-like flowers are white with a brilliant yellow ring around the purple eye and appear for a long period throughout the summer, especially if flowers are dead-headed or cut.

Cultivation

A sunny site in a reasonably fertile soil is best. 'Polar Star' will tolerate a dry site better than a very wet one. In wet or windy areas the plants may need discreet support from pea sticks; they do tend to flop in bad weather and in very rich soil.

Propagation

Sow the seed outside in spring and thin the seedlings out first to 1in (2.5cm), then 3in (7.5cm) and eventually to 12in (30cm) apart. Seed from the best plants can be saved for the following year.

Uses in the garden

A big group looks wonderful in a mixed or herbaceous border and they can also be grown in an annual border or in the vegetable garden for cutting.

Alternatives

There is also a wonderful mixture called 'Court Jesters', containing flowers in an exceptional range of colours.

Argyranthemum
'Jamaica Primrose'

Summer-flowering shrub
Half-hardy, to 2ft (60cm)

THIS IS a rounded shrub reaching 2ft (60cm) in height with coarse, slightly glossy foliage. The summer-long yellow daisies start off a rich butter-yellow and fade slightly as they age. Plants usually flower from early summer until the first frosts. The full name of this plant is *Argyranthemum frutescens* 'Jamaica Primrose' but it's also sometimes still listed under *Chrysanthemum frutescens*.

Cultivation

Plant out after the last frost in your area in reasonably fertile soil and full sun. In over-rich soil or with over-generous feeding, too much leaf and not enough flower are liable to be produced. 'Jamaica Primrose' also makes an excellent short standard plant for a large container.

Propagation

Although this is a shrub, it's not frost hardy so plants will not survive the winter unless protected. Cuttings can be taken in a gritty compost in early autumn and kept until spring in their cuttings pots in a greenhouse or conservatory which is just frost free. They should then be potted up. Pinch out when the plants are still quite small unless you want a standard, in which case remove the side shoots as they grow and retain the growing tip. Cuttings taken and potted up in autumn will make larger plants for planting out and so make bigger bushes by the end of the summer – but you need the space in the greenhouse. In heated conservatories and greenhouses cuttings taken a little earlier than suggested will make substantial plants and flower all winter.

Uses in the garden

'Jamaica Primrose' looks good as the main plant in a container or as a specimen plant in a bedding scheme. In groups of three or five between shrubs they are also very effective. Try them, too, in front of tall, lime-green nicotianas, behind dark-leaved fibrous begonias such as 'Coco Pink' or the slightly taller green-leaved 'Rusher Rose'. *Lavatera* 'Silver Cup' is also a very good companion.

Alternatives

'Vancouver' is a wonderful pink, anemone-

flowered variety which was almost the first choice; 'Quinta White', also known as 'Sark', is a white anemone-centred variety which is not yet generally available but worth looking out for, and the delightful *Argyranthemum foeniculaceum* has small white daisies with narrow grey foliage. There are others too, all good except the almost misshapen 'Double Yellow'.

Verbena
'Silver Anne'

Summer-flowering perennial
Half-hardy, to 12in (30cm)

THIS IS a verbena with oval, rather rough leaves and an attractive spreading habit. The pink flowers are carried in flat heads with many flowers in each one. The individual flowers are pale in the centre and, with their notched petals, create an attractive star-like effect.

Cultivation

Like so many bedding plants a sunny site and any reasonable soil seems to suit 'Silver Anne'. It thrives in heavy and light soils alike and, in well-drained sheltered spots, may well survive outside in the milder winters.

Propagation

Cuttings should be taken in late summer or early autumn and overwintered in the same way as argyranthemums (opposite). In anything but fairly spartan and cool conditions they grow all winter and it may be necessary to take more cuttings from the overwintered plants in spring in order to get shapely plants.

Uses in the garden

With their long spreading shoots, they're wonderful with a silver plant of similar habit, such as *Helichrysum petiolare*. In containers they mix well with other plants, their long shoots with their pink stars peeping through the foliage. They're good fillers among shrubs and in the front of mixed borders where they soften edges prettily. However, because of their spreading habit, it is best not to grow them in isolation as they can look rather bare of flowers in the centre of the plant.

Alternatives

There is a number of other old-fashioned

Argyranthemum
*'Jamaica Primrose' has
a long flowering season
– from early summer to
the first frosts. It is
handsome enough to
use as the focal point in
a bedding scheme.*

Impatiens 'Mother of Pearl' are among the best bedding plants for shade, the pale-coloured flowers gleaming brightly in dark corners. They will even survive under trees provided the soil is moist.

verbenas that are almost as good and are most certainly worth growing. 'Sissinghurst' is a much stronger pink and the cut leaves are prettier, 'Loveliness' is a good deep lilac, and 'Lawrence Johnston', also known as 'Huntsman', is brilliant scarlet.

Impatiens
'Super Elfin'

Spreading annual
Half-hardy, to 6–10in
(15–25cm)

THIS FLAT, spreading annual usually grows to little more than 6in (15cm) in the sun and no more than 10in (25cm) in shade. The plants have succulent leaves and stems with large, five-petalled flowers in an exceptional variety of shades. The colours range from the richest reds and purples through to the palest pastel lilacs and pinks. The mixture that is generally available contains 14 colours though more are on the way. The following separate colours are also available: deep red, orange, rich purple, salmon, deep lilac, shocking pink, soft lilac and white. A lovely mixture of soft, pastel colours from the 'Super Elfin' range is called 'Mother of Pearl'.

Cultivation
They will grow well in any reasonably water-retentive soil that is fairly fertile, although waterlogged sites are not suitable. They'll thrive in sun or shade.

Propagation
Seed should be sown in spring and covered very lightly with moist compost. The pots or trays can then be covered in opaque polythene and kept at a temperature between 70 and 75°F (21–24°C). Prick the seedlings out into trays or small pots and keep them fairly warm until hardening off time then plant out after the last frost. The seed can be temperamental and it's important to keep the temperature up. They're also susceptible to damping off so need careful watering. Germinated seedlings and young plants are generally available from seed companies.

Uses in the garden
Busy Lizzies are the best bedding plants for shade and I've found this variety to be the finest of all. The paler shades really brighten up dark corners, even under trees, if the soil is fairly moist. They're good in

tubs in shady courtyards or in window boxes on the cool side of the house. They'll also thrive in sunny sites as long as they don't dry out.

Alternatives
'Novette', sometimes known as 'Florette', is a good alternative though it grows taller. 'Accent' is probably the second best and 'Blitz' is the one to go for if you prefer a much taller, bushier plant.

Nemesia
'Mello'

Summer-flowering annual
Half-hardy, to 9–12in
(23–30cm)

AN IDENTICAL plant was grown in the 1950s under the name of 'Aurora' whilst names like 'St. George' and 'National Ensign' refer to the same plant. This new strain was developed from a single plant found in the 'Tapestry' mixture and introduced by Thompson and Morgan in 1989. It is a rather upright, relatively small-flowered nemesia reaching about 9–12in (23–30cm). The flowers start to appear in early summer and continue for many weeks, though they will be over by the autumn. The individual flowers, which densely cover the plants, come in a very striking combination, the upper petals being raspberry red and the lower ones pure white. The fact that 'Mello' won't flower right through the summer may be seen as a disadvantage, but it still flowers for longer than most perennials.

Cultivation

Grow them in a soil that retains moisture well, otherwise the flowering period may be dramatically curtailed as the plants dry up in the heat. They are happy in sun or light shade as long as they don't dry out.

Propagation

Sow the seed outside where the plants are to flower at any time in spring. Thin them to about 6in (15cm) apart. Alternatively, they can be sown in spring in a propagator, pricked out into trays and planted out in late spring.

Uses in the garden

'Mello' is a real show-stopper for containers and for gaps in beds and borders. Plan to follow it on with another plant for later in the summer.

Alternatives

'Tapestry' makes a similar plant but comes in an astonishing range of colours including some lovely blues. 'Carnival' has larger flowers but they are confined to reds, oranges and yellows.

Lunaria annua

Spring-flowering biennial
Hardy, to 2¹/₂ft (75cm)

DESPITE ITS Latin name, honesty is a biennial reaching 2½ft (75cm) in height, sometimes more. A bold rosette forms in late summer and in the following spring the flower stems appear and carry long, open heads of four-petalled purple flowers. These are followed by large round flat silvery pods.

Cultivation

Honesty thrives in a slightly shaded situation in soil that doesn't dry out too much.

Propagation

Seed should be sown outside in a seed bed in summer, thinned to 6in (15cm) and the seedlings transplanted to their flowering sites in autumn.

Uses in the garden

Honesty can be used formally as a spring bedding plant and bedded out with 'Golden Appledorn' tulips. Alternatively, plants can be set in a mixed border wherever there are a few gaps. If you allow them to self sow they will keep popping up year after year. The purple can clash unexpectedly when self-sown plants appear amongst other spring-flowering plants but this is really only a minor irritation. If you want the seed heads for drying, line a few plants out in the vegetable garden.

Alternatives

There's a lovely white-flowered form, and a beautiful rich purple variety called 'Munstead Purple' as well as a hideous variegated one, to be avoided at all costs.

Cheiranthus
'Blood Red'

Spring-flowering biennial
Hardy, to 18in (45cm)

THIS IS ONE of the taller wallflowers, reaching about 18in (45cm) in height. In spring the bushy plants produce large numbers of flower spikes lined with the deepest blood-red flowers. They have an exquisite scent, especially after a shower.

Cultivation

Most soils in sunny sites suit wallflowers, but limy soils are preferable to acid ones.

One of the taller wall-flowers, Cheiranthus *'Blood Red' looks good in association with tulips like 'White Triumphator' and the yellow 'West Point'. The scent is delightful.*

Strong winds can cause the plants to rock and so loosen the roots and this can lead to winter losses. A little shelter is helpful. The other option is to sow later and so plant out smaller plants. Like brassicas, wallflowers suffer from clubroot so if you choose part of the vegetable plot on which to raise them, grow them with the sprouts. And remember that if you raise the seedlings on infected soil, you'll probably spread the infection to your flower beds when you plant them out.

Propagation

Seed should be sown outside in early summer, thinned to 1–1½in (2.5–4cm) apart and then transplanted 6–9in (15–23cm) apart to grow on into strong bushy plants. If grown too close together, tall, spindly plants will result, giving fewer flowering shoots.

Uses in the garden

'Blood Red' looks good with a lily-flowered tulip such as 'White Triumphator' or the yellow 'West Point'. 'Primrose Bedder' wallflowers or 'Universal White' pansies could be used as an edging in front. 'Blood Red' is a little tall for smaller containers but is good in drifts amongst shrubs, as well as in more formal, organized spring schemes.

Alternatives

Other good varieties amongst the taller wallflowers are 'Fire King', 'Primrose Monarch' and 'Ivory White'. For edging and containers the 'Bedder' series, in yellow, primrose, orange and scarlet, is ideal.

Viola
'Universal'

Winter-flowering perennial
Hardy, to 6in (15cm)

THIS WINTER-FLOWERING pansy comes in 12 different colours and really does flower in the winter. It reaches about 6in (15cm) in height. The start of flowering depends a little on when the seed is sown but there should be flowers open in all but the fiercest periods of winter; then, come the spring, the colour is even better. 'Universal' pansies usually come as a mixture of single colours and bicolours. Eleven single colours are also available separately. The different colours may flower at different times through the season.

Cultivation

Good soil which is not too waterlogged suits them best, in either sun or partial shade. They will flower best in winter in a sunny, sheltered site.

Propagation

The seed is not cheap so it pays to sow in a tray in late spring or early summer, prick out into pots or trays and plant out in the autumn when pot-grown plants at least should be flowering.

Uses in the garden

They are wonderful in tubs and window boxes, in small beds and in the front of borders with small bulbs.

Alternatives

'Floral Dance' was the best winter-flowering type previously available and is still the best alternative.

comes when the plants are past their best anyway but it can be unsightly. Avoiding hot dry sites, making sure that the soil retains a little moisture (but is not badly drained) and spraying formal displays will help.

Propagation

Sow outdoors in early summer, thin out or transplant to grow on, then move the young plants to their final positions in the autumn. A fairly well-drained soil is a great help otherwise the plants can rot in wet spells.

Uses in the garden

This neat forget-me-not is a wonderful foil for tulips and wallflowers in spring and is also good for naturalizing in borders.

Alternatives

Other good varieties available include 'Blue Ball', reaching only 6in (15cm), 'Blue Bouquet' at 15in (38cm) and 'Blue Bird' at 2ft (60cm) – pick the variety that suits your purpose. There are also varieties in pinkish shades though these are not as good.

Polyanthus
'Crescendo'

Spring-flowering perennial
Hardy, to 8in (20cm)

SPECIALLY BRED for growing outdoors, 'Crescendo' grows to about 8in (20cm) and flowers in seven different colours – blue, red, rich pink, gold, rose pink, primrose and white. So far, only the blue has been available as a separate colour. Some of the colours are not uniform so beware if you have very precise ideas about colour combinations. The red, gold, primrose and white should be pure, but the two pinks and the blue are more accurately described as groups of similar shades. The flowers appear in dense heads at the tops of stout stems all through the spring.

Cultivation

Most reasonable soils in sun or partial shade suit polyanthus well but waterlogged soils may cause rotting. Moist but well-drained is the elusive ideal. Make sure container composts have good drainage or the compost may stay too wet in winter.

Propagation

Seed is best sown in late spring or early

Myosotis
'Ultramarine'

Spring-flowering perennial
Hardy, to 12in (30cm)

THIS DEEP ultramarine blue forget-me-not reaches about 12in (30cm) in height and flowers from early spring on rounded little plants.

Cultivation

A well-drained soil is a great help and it can pay to pot up a few spares and keep them in a cold frame if your soil is rather heavy. You will then have plants on hand to fill any gaps that may have appeared by the spring. A dry starved soil is not suitable.

Mildew can be a severe problem and there's no mildew-resistant variety available. They're especially prone to attack in hot, dry spells in spring. Often this attack summer after the summer bedding has been moved out of the greenhouse. Use a peat-based compost and don't cover the seed. Cover the pots with opaque polythene and keep out of direct sun at a temperature of 65°F (18°C) or just below. Higher temperatures may prevent germination. As soon as most of the seeds have started to show a tiny white root, sieve a little fine compost over the seedlings to help the roots anchor well. Prick out into trays, then move out into the cold frame when they're growing well. Pot up into 3½-in (9-cm) pots or grow on outside before planting out in the autumn.

Uses in the garden

These make excellent container plants and are very good in mixed borders, with dwarf tulips or grape hyacinths making good companions.

Bellis 'Pomponette' flowers profusely, with masses of tight, double daisy flowers in spring, and makes an excellent edging plant.

Alternatives

'Pacific Giants', 'Pacific Dwarfs' and other varieties will not usually make such robust plants and could suffer in bad winters, but the colour range may be better.

Bellis
'Pomponette'

Spring-flowering perennial
Hardy, to 6in (15cm)

THESE NEAT, spring-flowering daisies make compact rosettes of foliage and produce vast quantities of double flowers on short stems reaching no more than 6in (15cm) in height. The flowers come in just three shades, red, pink and white, though usually only a mixture is available. Occasionally some flowers which are not fully double may appear.

Cultivation

Any reasonable soil in a fairly sunny site seems to be suitable. Dead-heading helps prolong the display and fortunately a quick tug will pull off the flowers.

Propagation

Seed should be sown in late spring or early summer. It can be sown in a seed bed outside and the seedlings thinned out to 3–4in (7.5–10cm) apart before planting out in the autumn. Alternatively, sow the seed in pots in a cold frame, prick out into trays and then plant them out to grow on until transplanting them to where they are to flower.

Uses in the garden

These daisies make excellent edgers or small groups at the front of the border. They look good with small, later-flowering bulbs and make excellent window-box plants and are good in tubs too. 'Pomponette' tends to flower a little later than some of the other strains and so may still be going strong when the summer bedding needs to be planted out. However, plants like alyssum can be set behind them and will spread forward to cover the space when the daisies are removed.

Alternatives

'Kito' is a good fully double deep red. 'Goliath' is a big and blousy mixed strain, rather taller and a little untidy.

CONTAINER PLANTS

PLANTING IN tubs, baskets and window boxes gives you so many splendid opportunities to add to the interest and excitement of your garden that it's hardly surprising that this has been growing in popularity. At present, container gardening seems almost entirely restricted to growing spring and summer bedding in baskets and tubs, and alpines in troughs. But there's far more to container gardening than geraniums, lobelia and saxifrages.

You can grow plants which wouldn't normally tolerate your garden soil. Rhododendron lovers, for example, who garden on limey soils can fill large tubs with acid compost and so permit their favourite plants to thrive contentedly. Tubs also allow you to grow interesting and spectacular tender plants as they can be moved into a protected spot for the winter. The mobility of tubs also enables you to introduce colour temporarily to areas of the garden which are perhaps at their best at just one season and then need a little extra interest later.

All sorts of containers, especially baskets and window boxes, will brighten up the area around the house, where we all like to keep our garden at its most interesting for as long as possible.

There are three approaches to choosing plants for containers. You can pick permanent plants, tender or hardy, and leave them in place; you can change the display every spring and autumn using bedding and other dispensable plants; or you can keep one or two plants in permanently and slotting bedders into the gaps. A pot can be planted with just one variety, such as a specimen maple or a group of lilies. The pot can then stand alone or alongside others to form a group. Alternatively, a number of varieties in one container can form an attractive association.

Not only are there plenty of plants to choose from, but there are so many ways of dealing with them that, with a little imagination, you can create something really individual that suits your style of garden, matches your style of house and expresses your own personality.

In the following selection there's a mixture of the hardy and the tender, the permanent and the temporary. All are excellent container plants.

Pieris
'Forest Flame'

Evergreen shrub
Hardy, to 5ft (1.5m)

THIS IS a hybrid between *P. formosa forrestii* 'Wakehurst' and *P. japonica* which originated as a chance seedling in about 1946 at Sunningdale Nurseries in Surrey. It is a familiar and much-loved hardy evergreen shrub. It reaches 12ft (3.6m) in the garden but not usually more than about 5ft (1.5m) in a container. It has two chief attractions. Firstly, there's the bright red colouring of the young shoots as they burst into growth in the spring. This changes through pink and cream before finally turning green. Secondly, there are the flowers, like small lilies-of-the-valley in long branching strings.

Cultivation

This plant is a definite lime hater and so a special compost for lime-hating plants is required. A large container will be needed to give sufficient root room to encourage strong growth and to provide plenty of moisture. A site in partial shade will suit it well. For gardeners without suitable soil to grow this lovely plant, a container of lime-free compost is the only answer. Even then, iron deficiency can occur, especially if

Pieris 'Forest Flame' gets its name from the attractive, bright red young foliage, but it also has pretty lily-of-the-valley-like flowers later in the season.

watered with hard tap water. Treatment with sequestered iron will solve the problem. In dry conditions and in full sun, icy winds or late frosts the attractive young growth can be damaged. Half-shade and protection from the wind should be provided.

Propagation

Take cuttings 3–4in (7.5–10cm) long in late summer and root in a sandy, lime-free compost in a cold frame. Pot up the rooted cuttings in spring.

Uses in containers

It looks good in a tub by itself, although late in the season it couldn't be said to be the most attractive plant in the garden. I've seen it covered in the climbing flame flower, *Tropaeolum speciosum*, and that looks wonderful. Edging the pot with summer heathers can work, although they usually prefer rather more sun than the *Pieris* likes. A couple of variegated ivies, the silvery 'Glacier' perhaps, may be the answer.

Alternatives

There are a number of other good *Pieris*. 'Wakehurst', 'Jermyns' and 'Firecrest' are all worth looking out for.

Pelargonium
'Rouletta'

Colourful trailing plant
Tender, trailing to 18in (45cm)

I VY-LEAVED geraniums, whose natural antecedents grow wild in South Africa, have trailing stems carrying succulent, ivy-shaped leaves in shiny green. In 'Rouletta' the stiff stems carry heads of semi-double flowers in pure white, edged with a bold cerise margin.

Cultivation

Sunshine and a loam-based compost suit 'Rouletta' best although it will also thrive in peat-based composts. Although it's drought-resistant, dry conditions cause the lower leaves to drop and growth to slow up.

Propagation

Cuttings will root at almost any time but by taking them in late summer and overwintering them without potting on in a just-frost-free greenhouse, you can carry most

cuttings in the least space. In spring, pot them up, grow them a little warmer and take more cuttings from these young plants to encourage them to grow bushily.

Uses in containers

They are best planted round the edge of a container to trail down the sides and make a startling curtain of colour. Planted further back in a tub the stems will make their way to the front and the flowers will peep through the other foliage on the way. White petunias make good companions.

Alternatives

There's a huge range of ivy-leaved geraniums available with single, semi-double or double flowers; they can be vigorous and lanky or neat and compact. Some even have variegated leaves. I would especially suggest 'Amethyst' (lilac), 'La France' (mauve with darker streaks), 'Yale' (rich red), 'Snow Queen' (white), and 'Galilee' (pink).

Pelargonium 'Rouletta' is one of the best ivy-leaved trailing geraniums with its striking pink and white flowers. It looks good planted with white petunias.

Pelargonium
'Irene'

Splendid bedding geranium
Tender, to 12in (30cm)

B RED IN Ohio in 1942 and followed in the 1950s by similar varieties in other colours, this is a vigorous, red-flowered zonal pelargonium with fat, strong stems, large leaves, long stout flower stems and a large number of flowers per head. 'Irene' makes a big, bulky, well-branched plant, producing masses of flowers which fill tubs well.

Cultivation

'Irene' grows best in a John Innes compost and, being vigorous and leafy, appreciates more water and more generous feeding than other pelargoniums. The extra-leafy growth can be encouraged by too much nitrogen in the liquid feed. If this seems to be the case, switch from a general feed to a tomato feed.

Propagation

'Irene' can be treated in the same way as 'Rouletta'.

Uses in containers

Good as a single plant or in a group of three to fill a tub. With other plants in a big tub, making a colourful mixed group, it's excellent.

Alternatives

There are now a number of other colours in this 'Irene' type and I would suggest 'Penny' (lilac pink with a white centre), 'Party Dress' (soft pink) and 'Cardinal' (deep red). If you prefer geraniums raised from seed, then look out for 'Scarlet Diamond', 'Solo' and 'Century Scarlet'.

Acer palmatum
'Dissectum Atropurpureum'

Elegant deciduous shrub
Hardy, to 4ft (1.2m)

T HE WILD species comes from Japan and this is one of the most elegant and popular of its varieties. It is a slow-growing, twiggy shrub of rounded outline, eventually reaching about 4ft (1.2m) in

height and rather more across, though taking many years to do so. As the plant develops it becomes attractively symmetrical in outline. The foliage is very finely divided into feathered fingers of rich purple which turn attractive fiery shades in the autumn. Cut-leaved maples, being slow growing, are rather sparse in appearance in their early years and so, although the cost will be high, it's often a good idea to buy a good-sized specimen to start with.

Cultivation

This maple prefers a neutral or acid growing medium; a loam-based compost without the lime or a peat-based ericaceous compost is probably the best choice. The container should be positioned out of the sun and although dappled shade is ideal, it will do well in the shade of the house wall or fence. In full sun the plant is liable to dry out quickly and the leaves scorch. It's im-

Remember that if these are allowed to smother the young shoots of the maple, its shape may be spoiled.

Alternatives

There are a number of other attractive varieties. 'Dissectum' has fresh green leaves and good autumn colour and 'Dissectum Nigrum' is the darkest possible purple, but even slower growing.

Melianthus major

Foliage shrub
Tender, to 3ft (90cm)

THIS SLIGHTLY tender shrub is a native of South Africa and was introduced into Britain in 1688. It rarely survives outdoors in cold areas or hard winters. The attractive, slightly bluish grey foliage is divided like rose foliage, but is much larger and neatly toothed along the edges – a description which doesn't really do it justice. It doesn't produce many branches but the leaves are large and the whole effect is stunning. The flowers appear in narrow spikes with chocolate-brown bracts making a colourful narrow spike on growth from the previous year. Unfortunately this is the growth usually killed by frost.

Cultivation

It does best in large tubs or barrels in a loam-based compost. The tub must be moved into a porch or very sheltered spot outside, or into a greenhouse or conservatory for winter protection.

Propagation

It is not easy to propagate from cuttings, but seed has recently become available and this is the most reliable method.

Uses in containers

It is ideal as the main element in a large group of foliage plants. Good companions include the finely cut grey-leaved *Artemisia* 'Powis Castle', the trailing grey *Helichrysum petiolare* and its yellowish variety 'Limelight', the purple-leaved sage *Salvia officinalis* 'Purpurascens', and, for flowers, the big blue daisies of *Felicia* 'Santa Anita'.

Alternatives

There's nothing quite like this majestic foliage plant.

Acer palmatum 'Dissectum Atropurpureum' is one of the best of the Japanese maples for container growing, making an elegant, very small tree, whose foliage turns fiery red in autumn.

portant that the compost does not dry out and a large tub or barrel at least 2ft (60cm) across is preferable. Late spring frosts sometimes damage young foliage, but this is rare if the container is sited thoughtfully. No pruning should be necessary.

Propagation

Most plants are grafted and, as this is a technique that requires practice and skill, it's best left to the experts. Seed of dark-leaved maples is sometimes available from seed catalogues but the plants are slow to grow and may not be as good as grafted ones.

Uses in containers

This plant is definitely best as a single specimen in a large pot where its attractive foliage and form can be shown off to the best advantage. However, if it's planted in a large pot when still small the surrounding compost can be planted with temporary plants.

Helichrysum petiolare *'Limelight', with its striking lime-coloured leaves, makes an excellent foliage plant for containers planted up with, say, begonias or calceolarias.*

Helichrysum petiolare
'Limelight'

Foliage perennial

Half-hardy, to 18in (45cm)

A FORM of the wild species from South Africa, 'Limelight' is a half-hardy perennial grown for its arching, rather woolly shoots carrying furry, heart-shaped leaves in a delightful lemon-lime shade. These shoots can reach 2–3ft (60–90cm) in length in a single summer but the growth is not dense so the shoots insinuate themselves amongst other plants. Occasionally a plant may produce clusters of small yellowish everlasting flowers from white buds at the ends of the shoots.

Cultivation

It grows well in most composts and has a definite liking for full sun although it also thrives in open but shaded sites. In spite of the woolly covering to its leaves and stems, it's not a good survivor in drought so careful watering is necessary to prevent wilting and dropping of the lower leaves. Being a half-hardy perennial, it should not be set outside until after the last frost.

Propagation

Although hardier than, say, a dahlia, it will be killed in winter so cuttings should be taken in early autumn and rooted in a mixture of 50:50 peat and perlite. They can stay in their pots all winter in a greenhouse or conservatory which is just frost free, but if kept warmer should be potted up in the autumn. Otherwise pot up in spring and grow cool until planting.

Uses in containers

This is a good variety to peep through flowering plants. The lovely *Salvia patens* 'Cambridge Blue' is a good companion, as are the yellow daisies of *Argyranthemum* 'Jamaica Primrose'. It is good, too, with pendulous begonias, the rusty-coloured *Calceolaria* 'Kentish Hero' and around a dark-leaved canna, for example. It also makes a good standard.

Alternatives

The wild species is silver in colour and a most useful plant. There is also a variegated version, 'Variegatum'. The small-leaved, rather floppier variety once called *Helichrysum microphyllum* should now be known as *Plecostachys serpyllifolia* but in spite of its awkward name, this too is well worth growing but in its habit it is more of a trailer.

Yucca filamentosa

Architectural foliage plant
Half-hardy, to 6ft (1.8m)

THIS YUCCA grows wild in the south-east United States and was introduced to Britain in 1675. Its rounded, dense clumps of narrow, grey-green foliage are a year-round attraction, especially as the leaves are edged with twisting strings of creamy-white threads. This foliage makes a rounded plant about 18in (45cm) in height, without the tree-like stems of the more common *Yucca gloriosa*. In summer the flowers appear in conical heads on stems up to 6ft (1.8m) high. These heads are made up of large numbers of creamy-white bells and appear even on quite young plants.

Cultivation

A very large container is not required as the plants look best when the leaves just over-hang the edge of the pot. As they are not quick growing they can be re-potted every few years, increasing the size of the pot each time. The compost should be a soil-based one; peat-based composts hold too much water and yuccas like good drainage. They thrive in full sun and will tolerate a less than regular watering regime.

If grown in pots, where the roots can become sodden and frozen, yuccas may not survive the winter so it pays to move them into a greenhouse or conservatory, or a sheltered corner outside, during the winter months.

Propagation

Every so often suckers will appear at the base of the plant and when these have developed their own roots they can be detached and potted up separately.

Uses in containers

Yuccas are definitely most successful as specimen plants with no companions as their foliage will then be shown off to best advantage.

Alternatives

There is a yellow variegated variety, 'Variegata', and also a very impressive neat but less hardy species, *Y. whipplei*, with very fine, sharp pointed leaves in a good bluish grey shade.

Lobelia
'Sapphire'

Trailing annual
Half-hardy, to 6in (15cm)

A CULTIVATED form of a half-hardy perennial plant from South Africa, this plant is usually grown as a half-hardy annual. It is an old-established trailing lobelia with intense deep blue flowers, each with a white eye.

Cultivation

Grow it as a half-hardy annual and set outside after the last frosts. Any peat- or loam-

One of the best architectural plants for containers, Yucca filamentosa *makes an impressive mound of grey-green foliage with creamy edges.*

based compost suits it and it will be at its happiest in full sun. In slight shade it will tend to become drawn. It will not be happy in drought conditions.

Propagation

Plants are usually on sale in garden centres and, as the seed is so fine and difficult to sow, this might be the best source. If you'd like to raise them yourself, sow the seed in early spring. Sow on the surface of a moist, peat-based compost and cover the pot with clingfilm. Keep in a heated propagator until the seed is through and then keep in a warm place and don't let the young seedlings dry out. They are best moved on to trays or pots in small patches of seedlings as the seedlings are so small that they are impossible to handle individually.

Uses in containers

This lobelia is a splendid filler, billowing out from amongst other plants and airily filling any gaps to give a good, full-looking display. It can be used in the familiar red, white and blue combination with a pelargonium (geranium) like 'Irene' or 'Solo' and a white petunia such as 'White Joy'. The white eye links up the display and also helps if you intend to use it with softer shades.

One of the hardiest clematis, Clematis macropetala *produces masses of attractive light blue flowers in spring.*

Alternatives

There are a number of other good varieties. 'Blue Cascade' is soft Cambridge blue and there are also various ruby-like shades, some rather watery. 'Cascade Mixed' is an effective mixture.

Clematis macropetala

Blue-flowered climber
Hardy, to 3m (10ft)

THIS CLEMATIS grows wild in Siberia and northern China and was introduced to Britain in 1910. It is a fairly vigorous deciduous climber which clings by its leaf stems. The foliage is delicate for a clematis and in spring there are huge quantities of cool blue flowers, each with a pale centre. These are followed by fluffy seed heads. The likely cost of the large container required for this plant is usually its biggest drawback and its growth can sometimes be rather too vigorous.

Cultivation

A large container with a drainage hole is essential and this should be stood on a pair of tiles – one at each side – to allow free drainage. The compost should be loam-based with a layer of drainage material, such as coarse gravel, at the bottom. Watering with almost a gallon (4l) a day will be essential, and feeding with a low-nitrogen fertilizer during the growing season is important. To keep the roots cool, site the container in a fairly shady spot, not in direct sunlight.

After the first few years, growth is unlikely to be too rapid but shoots which have flowered can be cut back after flowering (the seed heads may have to be sacrificed).

Propagation

As with all clematis, layering is the simplest method of propagation. Simply peg a shoot that has reached the ground into a pot of good compost.

Uses in containers

Use a large, tall pot (an 'Ali Baba' jar is ideal) with netting fixed around it. The clematis can trail down from the top of the pot and will cling to the netting, thereby keeping it stable. When the flowers appear they stand out slightly from the foliage, making a delightful blue cape.

Alternatives

'Markham's Pink' and 'Snowbird' are self-explanatory varieties. For a plant that is less vigourous try one of the many varieties of *Clematis alpina*.

Impatiens
'New Guinea Hybrids'

Exotic annual

Tender, to 15in (38cm)

DEVELOPED FROM wild species growing in New Guinea, this makes an intriguing combination of foliage and flower colours for summer tubs. The plants are succulent, with a small number of rather thick stems and they are altogether more stout than the familiar bedding busy Lizzies.

The long oval foliage may be plain green, green with a yellow centre, green with a yellow edge, beetroot, beetroot and yellow or one of a number of other combinations. The flowers, which can be as much as $2\frac{1}{2}$in (6.5cm) across, are fewer than those of the bedding *Impatiens* and may be red, orange, pink, purple, lilac or white. The actual shades and the combinations of leaf and flower colour vary with the different strains available and seem to change from year to year as they are improved.

The best strains of these plants are raised from cuttings rather than seed and young plants in Jiffy 7 net pots are available from some of the seed companies.

Cultivation

'New Guinea' *Impatiens* make splendid plants for the conservatory and for containers in sheltered positions outside. They seem to thrive especially well in a peat-based compost but it's very important to ensure that the plants do not dry out. Although they will grow reasonably well in shade they can cope with plenty of sunshine as long as they are kept moist. If grown in a conservatory with a dry atmosphere or in a hot, dry place, red spider mite may well prove troublesome and often when this problem strikes, throwing the plants out is the best, if not the only, option. Being frost-tender, these plants must not be set outside until after the last frost and if you want to overwinter the plants a minimum temperature of 45°F (7°C) is advisable.

Propagation

Cuttings for overwintering root easily in late summer.

Uses in containers

They probably look their best planted as a mixture of colours without other plants, so their lustrous foliage and large flowers can be shown off without competition. Shading from other plants tends to cause the foliage to die off.

Alternatives

There are good 'New Guinea' types which are grown from seed, but so far these are only available in tangerine or a similar shade. 'Sweet Sue' is especially good in vermillion and is a wonderful conservatory plant; 'Tangeglow' is a very attractive soft tangerine. Both make especially spreading plants. The newer 'Tango' makes a more bushy plant.

Slightly stouter than most busy Lizzies, Impatiens 'New Guinea Hybrids' come in a wide range of colours and look best planted up as a mixture of colours, without other plants.

Laurus nobilis

Noble evergreen tree

Half-hardy, to 6m (20ft)

THE FAMILIAR evergreen herb, which grows wild in Mediterranean regions, makes a medium-sized tree when grown in the garden. In tubs, however, it can be kept to a neat pyramid, bun or lolli-pop shape by regular clipping. Growth generally tends to be fairly upright, the foliage is oval and glossy dark green and the stems are purple tinted.

Cultivation

Grow it in a relatively rich loam-based compost in a large tub or half barrel. Peat-based composts are not suitable. Feed and water regularly and stand in an open, sunny position. Prune to shape two or three times using secateurs during the growing season. In winter, especially in colder areas, bays in pots should be protected from cold winds and frost by moving the tub to a sheltered spot or cold greenhouse. Leaf scorch resulting from exposure to winter wind can destroy the appeal of the plant.

Propagation

Cuttings of side shoots about 4in (10cm) long, with a slight heel of older wood, can be taken in late summer and put in pots of sandy compost in a cold frame. Do not let them dry out. In spring they should have rooted and can be potted up.

Uses in containers

The bay is often used most effectively as a clipped specimen in the shape of a cone, bun, pillar or lollipop without other plants. Stationed like sentries at the foot of steps, outside doors and in similar positions they can be very effective.

In some parts of big cities, clipped bay trees (and box) in tubs are chained to railings to prevent their being stolen. Well-trained mature specimens are very valuable, so protect them accordingly.

Alternatives

The only other plant that is so amenable to such formal training is box.

Rhododendron
'Yellow Hammer'

Early dwarf rhododendron
Hardy, to 2ft (60cm)

THIS IS A hybrid between the very dwarf, upright-growing, primrose-yellow *Rhododendron flavidum* and the larger but more spreading *R. sulfureum*. It is a neat, rather upright-growing dwarf rhododendron with small foliage and pairs of bright yellow, bell-shaped flowers in large quantities at the tips and along the branches in spring. Occasionally some flowers may also appear in the autumn, though generally the flowering season is rather short.

Cultivation

Like *Pieris*, this is a plant for an acid compost and a large tub. Again, drought and scorching sun are the main enemies, although it tolerates sun better than most. Not quick growing, it still needs enough root space to develop without becoming pot bound, especially as once the roots fill the pot the compost dries out quickly. Tonics may be needed against iron deficiency, especially in hard water areas where tap water is used for watering.

Propagation

'Yellow Hammer' can be rooted in the same way as *Pieris* (see p 102).

Uses in containers

Being upright in habit, this variety makes an ideal plant for the back of a large tub and some even smaller rhododendrons can be planted round the edge. Three plants in a 2½-ft (75-cm) half barrel would be about right.

Alternatives

Other good dwarf varieties include the more compact, bright yellow 'Curlew', the creamy 'Dairy Maid', the white 'Bric a Brac' and the scarlet 'Humming Bird'.

One of the early dwarf rhododendrons, R. 'Yellow Hammer' makes a neat bush with a wealth of bright yellow bell-shaped flowers in spring.

ROCK & DWARF PLANTS

Tʜɪs ᴄʜᴏɪᴄᴇ of plants is likely to cause more controversy than most of my selections, especially as the experts on alpines tend to have such strong feelings about their favourite plants. This book is not written for fanatics, however. It's for keen, weekend gardeners and the plants selected are just brilliant.

It's often said that as gardens get smaller, people grow more small plants. Sometimes I think we just grow fewer plants, with the mixture of large and small much as before. In any case, it remains true that in a small garden, or indeed in any garden, the smaller the plants you grow the more you can fit in. This helps achieve the one thing that most gardeners demand these days – colour all the year round. Whether you go for mixed borders in which there's always something of interest or you set aside specific areas for specific seasons, small plants like these are an enormous asset in any garden.

For real alpine enthusiasts, the more difficult they are to grow, the better they like them. The result of this is that specialist nurseries list quite a lot of plants that most of us will find absolutely impossible to grow. They may only survive a matter of days after planting. So if you fancy growing a few more than those I recommend, read the catalogues carefully.

Euphorbia myrsinites

Front-of-border plant
Hardy perennial, to 6in
(15cm)

Tʜɪs ᴇᴜᴘʜᴏʀʙɪᴀ grows wild in rocky and dry grassy places in south east Europe. It is a prostrate plant lying more or less flat on the soil, with fat stems radiating from a central crown. Each stem is covered in spirals of narrow grey-blue leaves. In spring, showy heads of yellow flowers appear at the tips of the shoots and retain their attractiveness for some time.

An excellent plant for the front of a raised bed, Euphorbia myrsinites *has showy heads of yellow flowers in spring.*

Cultivation

This sun worshipper also revels in well-drained soil, though on the whole it's an accommodating plant. However, extremes of shade and wet soil will soon kill it and for the best flower heads and foliage colour, the most compact growth, sun and good drainage are essential. After the flowers finally lose their appeal the shoots which have carried them can be cut out entirely.

Propagation

Root cuttings of non-flowering shoots in late spring using a sandy compost.

Uses in the garden

An excellent plant for the front of a raised bed, it looks especially good with the stems growing out over a flat stone. It can also be positioned at the front of a border.

Alternatives

Euphorbia rigida is similar but has much shorter and narrower leaves and although very attractive is altogether less striking.

Helianthemum
'Wisley Pink'

Front-of-border plant
Evergreen shrub, to 9–12in
(23–30cm)

Oɴᴇ ᴏꜰ ꜰᴏᴜʀ well-established rock roses with the 'Wisley' prefix, 'Wisley Pink' is a small, twiggy, spreading evergreen shrub reaching about 9–12in

(23–30cm) in height with narrow grey leaves. The soft pink, five-petalled flowers appear in early summer and tone beautifully with the foliage.

Cultivation

Full sun is the most important requirement; good drainage is a big help but as long as the soil is not waterlogged there should be few problems. Clipping over as soon as the first flowers finish will not only help keep the plants bushy and dense but also encourage a second flush of flowers later in the year. Unpruned plants will become sparse and straggly.

Propagation

Cuttings can be rooted in summer if put in pots of sandy compost in a shaded cold frame.

Uses in the garden

Lawrence Hills, once an enthusiast for alpines and now a campaigner for organic gardening, recommended that a collection of helianthemums all be planted together in one bed. However, this needs plenty of space. 'Wisley Pink' is a great plant for the front of a sunny border where it can spread over a stone path or mowing edge without getting too rampant. It is good in a sunny silver border on heavy soil.

Alternatives

'Rhodanthe Carneum' is very similar but with darker pink flowers. 'Wisley Primrose', 'Wisley White' and 'Wisley Yellow' all have similar grey foliage.

Gentiana sino-ornata

Autumn-flowering gentian
Hardy perennial, to 6in
(15cm)

THIS EXCELLENT garden plant grows wild in China from where it was introduced shortly before the First World war. An autumn-flowering gentian, it is sometimes still flowering at the end of the year. It reaches about 6in (15cm) in height but the shoots spread from a central rosette to over 12in (30cm) in length. The upturned sparkling blue flowers appear at the ends of the shoots. They are tubular with a flared mouth and striped inside and out with dark blue and yellowish green.

Cultivation

This is one of the easiest gentians to grow, given the right conditions. The soil must be acid, the site shaded from the midday sun and the soil must not dry out, so plenty of organic matter is helpful.

Propagation

Small rosettes are produced during the growing season and these can easily be split off and replanted the following spring. It's sometimes said that plants grow and flower better if lifted and divided regularly.

Uses in the garden

This spectacular plant is best at the front of a bed where it can easily be admired. Erythroniums, trilliums and *Anemone nemerosa* make good spring plants for the same site. If your soil is not acid, it will thrive in a good-sized trough, though it must be kept moist. This gentian can be cut for the house as in good soil flowers are often produced in large quantities.

An autumn-flowering gentian, Gentiana sino-ornata *needs an acid soil which does not dry out and a site shaded from the mid-day sun.*

Alternatives

There is a white form of this plant and a delightful hybrid called 'Kingfisher' with darker foliage and larger flowers.

Campanula cochlearifolia
'Cambridge Blue'

Blue-flowered creeper

Hardy perennial, to 6in (15cm)

THIS IS A selected colour form of a species which grows wild in the European alps. It is sometimes listed as *C. pusilla*. Minute glossy green leaves creep delicately over the surface of the soil. Right through summer, usefully late for a good alpine plant, waving, wiry stems carry large quantities of tiny soft blue flowers about 4–6in (10–15cm) above the leaves. Although the tiny roots do run, this plant could never be described as a nuisance.

The blue-flowered creeper, Campanula cochlearifolia, *looks good set in between paving stones or at the front of a raised bed.*

Cultivation

Full sun and a well-drained soil are necessary but this is not a fussy or difficult plant. Slugs can sometimes be a problem though a good gritty mulch will always help; otherwise, resort to pellets.

Propagation

Rooted pieces can be detached and replanted in spring.

Uses in the garden

This campanula looks good in troughs, at the front of raised beds or rock gardens and is very useful to set between paving stones – as long as they've been laid on a sand base.

Alternatives

Over the years quite a number of colour forms have appeared. The white, 'Alba', is delightful, and a recently introduced neat blue double called 'Elizabeth Oliver' is a real treasure. 'Pallida' is a very pale blue and 'Oakington Blue' is about the darkest.

Viola
'Maggie Mott'

Misty blue violet

Hardy perennial, to 12in (30cm)

THIS VARIETY was probably introduced in the 19th century and was certainly popular by 1910. It is a vigorous plant making a large clump of juicy, fresh green shoots up to 12in (30cm) high with a tendency to sprawl. The sweetly scented flowers are very large in an exquisite soft lilac-blue with pale eyes and appear for a long period in spring and summer.

Cultivation

Sun and good drainage is ideal but a little shade and any reasonably cultivated soil should prove acceptable. Even in less than rich soils the growth can be lax and floppy and so easily beaten down by rain, wind or the weight of flowers and foliage. Slugs can also be a problem early in the season.

Propagation

Short cuttings only 1–2in (2.5–5cm) long can be taken from ground level in summer and inserted in pots of gritty compost in a shaded cold frame.

Uses in the garden

This viola looks wonderful with *Alyssum saxatile* 'Citrinum' (see below), and any other soft yellow colours and with silver foliage such as that of *Artemisia* 'Powis Castle'.

Alternatives

The number of good violets is huge, so I shall simply mention some of my favourites. 'Irish Molly' is a curious but beautiful greenish-olive shade though it's not as easy to keep as some of the others. The flowers on the exquisite 'Ardross Gem' are much smaller, in bright blue shading to a golden yellow eye. 'Molly Sanderson' has jet-black flowers, and 'Moonlight' is pale cream.

Alyssum saxatile
'Citrinum'

Soft-lemon-coloured spring favourite

Hardy perennial, to 9–12in (23–30cm)

The soft lemon-coloured flowers of Alyssum saxatile 'Citrinum' will tumble prettily over a wall in spring.

THIS IS A selected colour of the species which grows wild in southern and eastern Europe. Clumps of long, narrow, slightly greyish green leaves throw up dense clouds of tiny yellow flowers in a delightful pale lemon shade. It eventually makes 9–12in (23–30cm) in height. Flowering is in the second half of spring but the heads often flop unappealingly rather than cascade delightfully, in wet seasons or when grown in rich soil.

Cultivation

This reasonably tolerant plant will give its best in a sunny site with a well-drained soil that is not too rich. Dead head as soon as flowering is over.

Propagation

Cuttings of young shoots can be taken in early summer and rooted in a sandy compost. After potting up they can be grown on and planted out the following spring. Seedlings will usually appear but, if left to self sow rather than dead headed you'll probably find that many of the seedlings will not be quite the same shade.

Uses in the garden

It is good at the top of a low dry stone wall and the colour of limestone or pale sandstone sets off the flower colour well. It can also be planted amongst the rocks while the wall is being built. It looks especially good with soft blue flowers.

Alternatives

There are other colours. The natural species is a rather bright yellow; 'Plenum' is shorter and the double flowers last a little longer; though they're brighter than those of 'Citrinum'. 'Dudley Neville' is apricot. 'There is also one with variegated foliage which appeals to collectors of monstrosities', says alpines expert Will Ingwersen, but Beth Chatto says it 'forms a striking contrast among silver plants'.

Hebe
'Pagei'

Silvery-leaved carpeter

Compact shrub, to 12in (30cm)

THIS HEBE was first recorded in the botanic garden at Dunedin, South Island, New Zealand in 1926 where Edward Page, an emigrant from Sussex was foreman. *Hebe pinguifolia* is thought to be one of its parents and it is often found listed under this name. 'Pagei' is a low-growing, widely spreading shrub with reddish-brown branches and twigs. Its maximum height is about 12in (30cm), though is usually less, and it can spread to 3ft (90cm). The small leaves are bluish grey and turn to present their flat surfaces to the light. Short spikes of white flowers about 1in (2.5cm) long appear on the stem ends in late spring.

Cultivation

This is an amenable plant that thrives in a sunny position if planted in reasonably well-drained soil. It makes the most shapely bush in drier conditions.

Pruning is not usually necessary although there is a tendency for the older branches near the centre to lose their leaves and not produce enough new shoots to complete the cover of foliage. Thoughtful pruning combined with liquid feeding and watering can sometimes promote new growth. The foliage of bulbs grown underneath often accelerates leaf loss.

Propagation

Branches often root into the soil where they touch and this can be encouraged by pinning some down with stones. When rooted they can be detached and planted elsewhere.

Pulsatilla vulgaris 'Rubra', with its nodding rich-red flowers and feathery foliage is wonderful in a raised bed or rock garden.

Uses in the garden

A fine flat carpeter for raised beds, the edge of the border or even large troughs, 'Pagei' also looks good with short grasses. Beware of planting dwarf bulbs to grow up through it as their foliage will accentuate the tendency to lose leaves.

Alternatives

There is a number of other flat growing, small-leaved, silvery hebes including *H. pimeloides* 'Quicksilver', a rather more dome-shaped plant with narrow leaves and purple flowers, and *H. albicans* with much larger leaves and, again, a more mounded habit but with an impressive flowering display in summer. A prostrate form of *H. albicans* usually listed as 'Prostrate Form', has much lower, more spreading growth.

Pulsatilla vulgaris
'Rubra'

Pasque flower

Hardy perennial, to 12in (30cm)

THE NATURAL species is a rare British plant restricted to just a few sites on shallow limestone soils. This is a selected colour form originating on the

continent where the plant is more common and a number of other colours have also arisen. This dark, rich-red-flowered form of the Pasque flower produces silky bells in spring above finely cut foliage, each bell centred with bright yellow. Later the foliage expands into a slightly downy, feathery mound and the flowers give way to large, fluffy, dirty-white seed heads.

Cultivation

Full sun and a well-drained soil are again the simple requirements and if the soil is limy, so much the better. Once planted it's best left to increase without disturbance.

Propagation

If you collect your own seed and sow it straight away in a well-drained compost and leave it outside you will get quite good results. The flower colour of the seedlings may vary slightly.

Uses in the garden

This is a wonderful plant for a raised bed or rock garden where it's easy to turn up the nodding bells to look at the brilliant yellow boss inside.

Alternatives

The wild species is rich purple and there are also pink, red and lilac varieties, some attached to other species such as *Pulsatilla alpina* and *P. halleri*. Seed mixtures are also available and I'd suggest selecting plants in flower and looking for the best colour and the most vigorous growth.

Daphne cneorum
'Eximea'

Scented trailing plant
Evergreen shrub, to 6–9in
(15–23cm)

P ICKED OUT from a batch of plants by the plantsman A. T. Johnson in the 1930s, this closely resembles some wild forms of the species from south west France. It is a flat, spreading evergreen shrub with narrow, deep green leaves and may eventually reach 3ft (90cm) across though only 6–9in (15–23cm) high. The clusters of flowers appear at the tips of the shoots in late spring. The buds are deep red and open to rose-pink flowers with a lovely scent.

Cultivation

This is not an easy plant to grow. A well-drained soil is important but not one which dries out; it needs to capture that elusive combination of water retention and good drainage. Plant a young plant that is not pot bound and is grown in a loam- rather than a peat-based compost and, as it grows older, work in fresh peaty compost around the branches. Pegging down the branches to encourage rooting also helps keep the plant healthy. No pruning is usually required, except to pinch young plants out early to encourage a good habit and also to snip off any sickly or dead shoots.

Propagation

Take cuttings 2–4in (5–10cm) long in mid summer and insert in a sandy compost. Pot up and overwinter in a cold frame for planting out in spring.

Uses in the garden

This is a splendid plant for the rock garden, the larger raised bed or borders in which the appropriate soil conditions can be provided. Be prepared to give it space as if it thrives it might even make 6ft (1.8m) across.

Alternatives

There's nothing quite like 'Eximea' but you may be interested in the variegated variety with pale pink flowers, 'Variegata'.

Not the easiest of plants to grow, if treated well Daphne cneorum will make a spreading bush with clusters of fragrant rose-pink flowers in spring.

The deep blue buttercup-like flowers of Hepatica nobilis *make it a delightful plant for the shady side of a shrub at the front of a border.*

Hepatica nobilis

Spring-flowerer for the shade garden

Perennial, to 6in (15cm)

THIS SMALL perennial grows wild in most of mainland Europe except for the extreme north and extreme south. It forms a tight crown from which, in early spring, grow slender stalks carrying buttercup-like flowers in deep blue. Very dark green, kidney-shaped leaves appear with the last flowers. Sometimes these leaves are attractively mottled.

Cultivation

It grows best in a soil with plenty of organic matter which does not dry out and in a site which is at least partially shaded. It is best left undisturbed to encourage the most prolific flowering.

Propagation

Old clumps can be split and replanted but they do not generally respond well to such upheaval and take some time to recover. Seed can also be collected from your plants and sown in pots outside at once. Plants will take some time to reach flowering size.

Uses in the garden

This is a delightful spring plant for the shady side of a shrub towards the front of the border where its charm can best be appreciated.

Alternatives

There are also pink and white forms available and some very rare doubles which are almost never listed in catalogues.

Dianthus
'Pike's Pink'

Dwarf pink with large double flowers

Hardy perennial, to 3in (7.5cm)

THIS VARIETY was raised in the early 1960's by Mr J. Pike of Pike's Peak Greenhouses in Acton, south west London and given the RHS Award of Merit in 1966. The Pike's Peak nursery gave its name to a range of other pinks, that have now vanished. This variety makes a very neat plant no more than 3in (7.5cm) high. Greyish green cushions of narrow foliage make interlocking mats carrying exceptionally large, double pink flowers on short stems to create a very impressive show. It's very free flowering and also tolerates moisture in winter better than many of the other dwarf pinks.

Cultivation

A sunny site in well-drained soil, preferably with some lime in it, suits 'Pike's Pink' perfectly well and so it grows happily with many of the other easy-to-please rock plants. Take care not to allow neighbouring plants to smother it. Regular division and re-planting will help keep it vigorous.

Propagation

Dividing the plant every two or three years in spring will usually yield spare plants for replanting or potting up.

Uses in the garden

This is a wonderful plant for the front of raised beds and for larger troughs.

Alternatives

The range of dwarf pinks is very large. Even smaller than 'Pike's Pink' is 'La Boubrille' at 2in (5cm) high. It has sweetly scented pale pink, fringed flowers on grey foliage. There's also the white 'La Boubrille Alba' and both are definitely only for troughs. 'Little Jock' has silvery foliage and semi-double pink flowers with dark eyes.

Cheiranthus
'Bowles Mauve'

*Free-flowering shrubby
wallflower*

Perennial, to 2ft (60cm)

THIS PLANT, sometimes listed under *Erysimum* rather than *Cheiranthus*, is one of many plants with the name of E. A. Bowles attached to it. It's a hybrid, probably with some *Cheiranthus scoparius* and/or *C. linifolius* blood in it but no-one seems entirely sure how it came about. It is a perennial wallflower with fat but hard stems and long narrow leaves in an unusual shade of grey with a slight purplish tint at the base. It branches well from low down and makes a rounded, dome-like bush of foliage with the flower stems standing up from it well. The flowers are, as you might guess, mauve and appear in long spikes and for a long season from spring well into summer. In mild winters, and if dead headed earlier in the year, flowers may appear in the winter months too.

This short-lived plant will last three years at most. This is partly because it exhausts itself by flowering so prolifically and partly because the root system is poor. Wind rocks the roots and in winter wet soil rots them. Snow and rain can break the branches. It's common to see plants with all the branches splitting away near the base. Fortunately, they root very easily from cuttings.

Cultivation

This is another plant for a sunny, well-

The perennial wallflower, Cheiranthus 'Bowles Mauve', *has unusual grey leaves and often flowers for most of the year.*

drained site – indeed good drainage is crucial. Shelter from the wind is also a useful factor to bear in mind. Brush off any snow which settles on the plant in winter otherwise its weight can cause the branches to split apart at the base and death usually follows. Pruning is not usually necessary – or successful if you cut into old wood. Sometimes you will see the flowers streaked with fine cream lines and this is a symptom of virus infection. Usually this seems to have few other effects.

Propagation

Cuttings about 4in (10cm) long with the leaves stripped from the bottom half root almost all the year round. Late summer is the best time and will provide neat plants which can be overwintered in pots and planted in spring.

Uses in the garden

'Bowles Mauve' can be used as a spring bedding plant and white tulips make perfect companions. As a dwarf shrub; its unusual foliage and prolific flowering make it invaluable. It is a splendid small garden plant and a useful winter cut flower.

Alternatives

There is a number of other perennial wallflowers worth growing. 'Bredon', with deep red buds and bright yellow flowers, has the rounded habit and fat stems of 'Bowles Mauve' but its foliage is greener. Unfortunately this is not easy to find.

Berberis thunbergii
'Atropurpurea Nana'

Dwarf purple berberis
Hardy shrub, to 18in (45 cm)

RAISED IN Holland in 1942, this compact little plant is a reduced version of the familiar purple berberis (see page 65) that is often seen in massive groups, giving a depressing air to old overgrown shrubberies. Like its larger cousin, when used well this is a lovely little plant. It is slow growing and eventually reaches 18in (45cm) in height with a rather wider spread and is clothed all season in small rounded purple leaves. By this stage it is sometimes rather open and straggly but usually with some character. The fiery autumn colour is very good too.

Cultivation

A sunny site suits it best but although usually grown in well-drained soil this is a fairly tolerant little plant. A small amount of careful shaping may be necessary.

Propagation

Take 3–4-in (7.5–10-cm) cuttings of side shoots in late summer and root in a sandy compost in pots in a cold frame. Pot up in spring and plant out in autumn.

Uses in the garden

It is often used as a specimen in raised beds and rock gardens where attractive slow-growing shrubs with long seasons are not common. It also makes a good dwarf hedge.

Alternatives

'Bagatelle' is even tinier, reaching only 12in (30cm) and making a tight rounded hummock.

Helichrysum bellidioides

Creeping strawflower
Hardy perennial, to 4 in (10cm)

THIS CREEPING strawflower grows wild in New Zealand. It makes mats about 2ft (60cm) across, rooting as it goes, but only reaching a height of a few inches. The downy stems are white and the leaves are dark green. The small 'everlasting' flowers are creamy white and cover the plant in early summer.

Cultivation

This unusual plant thrives in a warm, sunny site in a well-drained soil where it will spread well. However, it can sometimes be too vigorous for more delicate neighbours.

Propagation

Rooted shoots can be detached and replanted in spring.

Uses in the garden

A wonderful low carpeter for a sunny bank or large rock garden, it can be underplanted with dwarf bulbs.

Alternatives

None.

BORDER PERENNIALS

YEARS AGO the herbaceous border was the great glory of many a British garden. You can still see splendid examples at such gardens as Newby Hall in Yorkshire and Jenkyn Place in Hampshire. In most gardens, herbaceous perennials are now grown in mixed borders with shrubs, bulbs, bedding plants and climbers as this enables gardeners to create a year-round succession of colour and interest; a border made up entirely of perennials can be singularly uninteresting at certain times of the year.

This change is reflected in the choice of plants grown and so my selection of the best of all perennials is made with the modern mixed border very much in mind. These may be a little less flamboyant but will have other fine qualities that make them especially valuable in the mixed border setting. I've also had in mind qualities like resilience, ease of propagation and whether plants are self supporting.

Some old favourites from the days of the traditional herbaceous border are included but there are also some which have come to prominence recently.

Anemone hybrida
'Honorine Joubert'

Long-flowering white anemone
Hardy perennial, to 5ft (1.5m)

INTRODUCED IN about 1858, this variety arose in France as a sport of *Anemone × hybrida*, a hybrid created by crossing the Chinese *A. hupehensis* with *A. vitifolia* from Nepal. The tall straight stems, reaching 5ft (1.5m) above low-level dark green foliage, carry a long succession of pure white flowers. Each flower is complemented by a brilliant yellow centre. 'Honorine Joubert' flowers for three months,

starting in late summer and so is at its best at a time when other plants in the garden are fading away.

Cultivation

A sunny site makes all the difference to the flower power of this wonderful plant. It grows well in most soils, but the heavier soils seem to suit it best and prevent it getting too invasive. It may take a little while to settle down after planting but once established it rarely needs lifting and dividing.

Propagation

The roots should be divided in spring. They are thick and woody and it pays to dig deep and extract a substantial chunk. Nevertheless, in the first season after replanting, the foliage may be small and the flower stem short. Alternatively root cuttings of the thicker, fibrous roots, about 2in (5cm), long can be taken in spring, potted up and planted out the following spring.

Uses in the garden

Place it in a position where you can see the clouds of white flowers easily. As it will not need splitting every few years, you can plant bulbs amongst the roots – snowdrops and aconites can be left to spread and self sow. If you want to make a white corner, add these anemones for their late show with artemisias and white tobacco plants. They also look good with the lavender Michaelmas daisy featured later in this selection.

Alternatives

There's a number of other varieties, the simplest being a good pink usually known just as *A. × hybrida*. There are also more dwarf types.

Anemone hybrida *'Honorine Joubert' flowers in late summer and early autumn when many other plants are past their peak.*

Delphinium
'Blue Nile'

Dramatic border perennial
Hardy, to 5–6ft (1.5–1.8m)

THE GARDEN hybrids are mainly descended from the tall Swiss species, *D. elatum*. 'Blue Nile' was raised by Blackmore and Langdon, who raised so many good varieties over the years. It is an impressive, traditional blue variety with a white eye, reaching about 5–6ft (1.5–1.8m) in height. It flowers in early summer and is a relatively healthy and robust variety that, unlike some less long-lived varieties, is also a good garden plant.

Cultivation

Most delphinium hybrids thrive best in a rich and fertile soil, although this can be improved clay or improved sand. Delphiniums do not root deeply so double digging is not necessary. Reasonable drainage is necessary so fork grit into the heaviest soils.

Sun suits them best but they will also do well in an area shaded by a wall or fence though the flower spikes may be rather more open. Under trees they will not thrive. Removing the first spikes as they fade will encourage more flowers to come later.

Support is essential in all but the most sheltered spots. This can be provided by tying each flower stem to a bamboo cane, with canes and string or by using a wire mesh frame. Mildew can be a problem with most delphiniums especially after flowering, though 'Blue Nile' is less susceptible than some. Regular spraying with a fungicide containing benomyl will help.

Propagation

Short cuttings about 4in (10cm) long, taken very early in the year, can be rooted in jars of water with gravel in the base. The base of the cutting sits on the gravel, covered with about 1–2in (2.5–5cm) of water.

Uses in the garden

The summer garden is not over-supplied with blues, so delphiniums are an essential constituent. They are best planted towards the back of the border so that later-flowering plants can grow up in front and hide the less-than-attractive foliage after flowering. However, if placed too near a hedge, fence or shrub they may lean precariously.

Alternatives

The older cuttings-raised varieties like 'Blue Nile' are not easy to come by but are well worth hunting out. Seed-raised types are much easier to find but are less long-lived and have less elegant flower spikes. 'Blue Jay' is fairly close to 'Blue Nile' and easier to find. The new seed-raised 'Pink Dream' looks good.

Dramatic plants for the back of a border, hybrids of Delphinium elatum *are the most widely grown. They need support in all but the most sheltered spots.*

Helenium
'Coppelia'

Autumn-flowering perennial
Hardy, to 3ft (90cm)

ONE OF A range of hybrids of two species from eastern North America – *Helenium bigelovii* and *H. autumnale* – this is a valuable perennial plant

Primula pulverulenta –
*the candelabra primula
– originates in China
and is particularly
popular for planting in
drifts at the water's edge.*

reaching about 3ft (90cm) in height. The stems are stiff and upright and in early autumn carry branching flower heads with large numbers of daisy-like flowers in gingery orange, each with a striking eye.

Cultivation

This is a very tolerant plant, thriving in any open situation in soil that is not water-logged. The weight of the flower heads is too much for even the stout stems to support so staking is usually necessary. This is also a fairly vigorous plant and the roots soon become congested.

Propagation

The roots can be divided every couple of years; the best pieces can be replanted, the next best given away or used for new clumps, and the tough woody material can be discarded.

Uses in the garden

'Coppelia' looks good with other fiery shades like crocosmias, pale yellows like *Argyranthemum* 'Jamaica Primrose' and yellowish or fresh green foliaged shrubs.

Alternatives

The shorter, mahogany-coloured 'Crimson Beauty' flowers a little earlier while the taller, later-flowering 'Riverton Beauty' (yellow with a maroon eye) is also good.

Primula pulverulenta

'Candelabra primula'

Moisture-loving perennial

Hardy, to 18in (45cm)

THIS SPECIES grows wild in the hills of west Szechuan in China and was introduced from there in 1905. It is a short-lived perennial with a rosette of fresh green foliage. From this arise tall straight stems covered in white meal and carrying several tiers of flowers. These flowers, which appear in early summer, are crimson with a dark eye.

One of the problems with candelabra primulas is their tendency to cross with each other to produce a range of colours. If you want to keep the colour pure, just grow the one candelabra.

Cultivation

A damp site is needed by this species and it thrives along stream sides or on the banks of ponds. However, water is not necessary to its well being though the soil must not dry out. It must also be rich and fertile and preferably in full sun or at most half shade.

The plants tend to be short-lived so if they don't self sow, they may die out. Virus can also be a problem; the leaves go rather yellow and sharp teeth develop along the leaf edges. Burn all infected plants.

Propagation

Plants can be divided after flowering, though they must not be allowed to dry out. When plants are happy, self-sown seedlings will appear nearby and these can be transplanted to other parts of the garden where you want them.

Uses in the garden

On the waterside it associates well with other primulas, though it should be kept away from other candelabra types to avoid hybrid seedlings. Other suitable companions include trilliums, hostas, various irises and ferns. This plant also looks good in front of rhododendrons but you must choose your colours carefully.

Alternatives

There is a pink-flowered variety called 'Bartley Strain' but for a similar shade the best bet is *P. japonica* 'Miller's Crimson'. The most obvious difference is that in *P. japonica* there is no white meal on the stems.

Phlox
'Border Gem'

Indispensable border plant
Hardy, to 3ft (90cm)

THIS OLD variety is an especially strong-growing, traditional border phlox raised many years ago. It reaches about 3ft (90cm) in height with flowers in a very striking bluish violet.

Cultivation

Phlox are easy-going plants but thrive in a fertile soil that is at least fairly well drained, although the extremes of solid clay or pure gravel are unlikely to produce fine plants. They flower best in full sun. Staking is not usually necessary. The foliage is unremarkable so to help hide it some gardeners cut back the shoots at the front of the group so that a few flower spikes are carried a little lower than the rest and hide the stems.

Propagation

Border phlox can suffer from stem eelworm which shows as twisted foliage. Plants are best dug up and burned and new phlox plants put in a different site. Plants grown from cuttings from diseased plants will carry the infection and, of course, by divid-ing clumps you simply spread the infection around. Those grown from root cuttings will be healthy. Equally, in the garden, pulling the clumps apart and replanting in spring works perfectly well with healthy plants.

Uses in the garden

This is a splendid plant for the traditional herbaceous border or in front of climbing roses in pink or white.

Alternatives

Other good varieties include the taller 'Balmoral' in pale pink, the shorter 'Branklyn' in deep lilac, 'Eva Cullum' in pink with a dark eye and 'Fujiyama' in pure white.

Geranium endressii
'Wargrave Pink'

Ground-covering hardy cranesbill
Evergreen, to 18in (45cm)

THE ORIGINAL species grows wild in the Pyrenees where it is becoming quite rare. 'Wargrave Pink' arose on the Waterers' nursery in 1930 and was found there by their foreman. It is a determinedly spreading plant with dense growth reaching up to 18in (45cm) in height with fresh, evergreen foliage. The upwards-facing

The hardy cranesbill, Geranium endressii 'Wargrave Pink' thrives in sun or shade and flowers over a long period.

flowers appear in early summer, last well into the autumn and are an attractive bright salmon pink.

Cultivation

This hardy cranesbill thrives in sun or shade, but grows slightly taller in the shade. Most reasonable soils suit it and indeed it's altogether a most adaptable plant, even making a brave show in dry shade.

Propagation

Plants can be divided either in spring or autumn.

Uses in the garden

'Wargrave Pink' makes an attractive and long-flowering plant, first coming into flower with the red weigelas with which it makes a splendid combination. It is good with blue and purple irises too.

Alternatives

G. endressii is the parent of a number of hybrids including 'A. T. Johnson', the result of a cross with G. versicolor, and over which there has been some confusion about the name; it has slightly darker salmon pink flowers. 'Claridge Druce' is another, rather taller hybrid of the same parentage with rosy pink flowers. These hybrids are the best alternatives but 'Wargrave Pink' is the most widely available.

Achillea
'Moonshine'

Yellow-flowered yarrow
Hardy, to 2ft (60cm)

S ELECTED BY Alan Bloom at Bressingham Gardens from a batch of mixed seedlings grown from seed collected from three older varieties, this yarrow is a vigorous plant with feathery grey-green foliage which lasts well through the winter. The flat heads of pale yellow flowers appear in early summer on stems about 2ft (60cm) high. 'Moonshine' has a tougher constitution than some achilleas and a more generous display of flowers.

Cultivation

Any reasonably fertile soil that is fairly well-drained is suitable and full sun encourages the best flowering. A. 'Moonshine' will not thrive in wet soil and won't flower in the

Achillea 'Moonshine' is a pale yellow yarrow, and makes an excellent back-of-the-border filler.

shade but otherwise is relatively trouble free. Clumps usually increase well and should be divided regularly to keep the plants neat and flowering well.

Propagation

Division yields many spare pieces of root, and shoots can be easily rooted as cuttings in spring.

Uses in the garden

This is a good foil for purplish plants such as *Salvia officinalis* 'Purpurascens' and cool blue campanulas and it looks surprisingly good with pink roses. It can be set at the front of the border and trimmed back firmly after flowering in which case you'll be blessed with a fine feathery mound of foliage for the rest of the season. Alan Bloom mentions that the foliage of some varieties is much appreciated by finches as nest material but I haven't found this to be a problem with 'Moonshine'.

Alternatives

Achillea taygetea has greener foliage and slightly more intense flowers; 'Flowers of Sulphur' is similar. The newer 'Great Expectations' has sandier flowers and is the most vigorous of the recently introduced 'Galaxy' hybrids which also include a red, a salmon and a weaker soft pink.

Aster × frikartii
'Mönch'

A good long-flowering plant
Hardy, to 3ft (90cm)

RAISED IN Switzerland around 1920 by crossing the violet *A. amellus* and the lilac *A. thompsonii*, this was the best of three seedlings named after famous mountains and the only one to survive. Less exciting seedlings sometimes masquerade under this famous name but even these will be good. Buy from a reliable nursery to get the real thing. It is a long-flowering plant, blooming for many months from mid summer onwards. It reaches about 3ft (90cm) and carries elegant, soft-lavender blue sprays of beautifully proportioned daisies with narrow rays and small yellow centres.

Cultivation

This plant deserves good soil and a sunny site and thrives if divided about every three years. It is fairly trouble free, needing little staking unless overfed, and rarely suffers from mildew.

Propagation

Divide the old plants in spring, discarding as much of the tough, older wood as possible. Replant the most vigorous pieces. Young shoots can also be rooted as cuttings in late spring.

Uses in the garden

It looks excellent with autumn sedums and in front of white anemones or those pink roses which are still flowering well right into the autumn.

Alternatives

Plants without the 'Mönch' varietal name are still good, and the varieties of one of the parents, *A. amellus*, such as 'King George' are well worth growing.

Aster × frikartii 'Mönch' is another long-flowering perennial, the elegant lavender-blue flowers blooming from mid summer onwards.

Astilbe
'Sprite'

Neat front-of-border plant
Hardy, to 15in (38cm)

THIS IS one of a group of dwarf varieties resulting from crossing existing garden hybrids with the very dwarf *A. simplicifolia*. A neat and densely growing dwarf astilbe, it reaches only about 15in (38cm) in height. The well-cut foliage is deep blue-bronze in colour and is over-topped with short, branching open spikes of fluffy rose pink flowers in late summer. Growth can be slow especially in dry soil, but this does not mean that the plant is ailing in any way.

Cultivation

'Sprite' is happy in most soils that are not

The lenten rose, Helleborus orientalis, *is one of the most attractive perennials with evergreen divided leaves and delicate drooping cup-shaped flowers in a range of colours from white to dark purple.*

too crisply drained. The addition of some organic matter helps in most situations. In dryish sites grow it in partial shade, otherwise full sun is best. A shortage of moisture in summer is the biggest threat.

Propagation

In spite of its slow growth, division of the roots in spring or autumn will slowly enable you to build up a good stock of plants.

Uses in the garden

'Sprite' makes a good edging plant, and is effective with roses. For a foliage contrast, grow it with *Lamium* 'Beacon Silver'.

Alternatives

Other dwarf varieties worth trying are 'Bronze Elegance', with a slightly salmony tint and the creamy 'William Buchanan'.

Salvia superba
'Lubecca'

Tough, long-flowering border plant
Hardy, to 18in (45cm)

THIS DWARF bushy plant reaches about 18in (45 cm) in height with long, dense spikes of purple flowers from early summer onwards. After the flowers

fade, the purple colouring in the spikes ensures the plants remain attractive for many more weeks.

Cultivation

An easy plant to grow, it thrives on most soils that have been even modestly improved, though it does best in full sun. If you cut the flowering spikes back immediately after flowering there is sometimes a second flush.

Propagation

Divide the plants in spring or take cuttings of the young spring shoots.

Uses in the garden

Dwarf enough for the front of the border, it will spread out to mask the border edge but will not usually collapse, even without staking. It looks good with *Achillea* 'Moonshine', lady's mantle and hardy geraniums. Dwarf bulbs can be planted amongst the clumps for early colour.

Alternatives

There are a number of similar varieties including the slightly taller 'East Friesland' and the larger-flowered 'May Night'.

Helleborus orientalis

Hardy raised-border perennial
Evergreen, to 12–18in (30–45cm)

THE LENTEN ROSE grows wild in Russia and Turkey and is an evergreen perennial with glossy, divided leaves, making good ground cover, from which rise upright stems about 12–18in (30–45cm) tall. These usually bear white flowers from about mid winter onwards, depending on the season. There are also pinks, purples, creams and even pale yellows and some forms are attractively spotted inside.

There is a lot of interest in breeding new varieties of this hellebore at present with special emphasis on yellow-flowered varieties. These are available from a number of specialist nurseries in two forms – seedlings and divisions. Seedlings are less expensive but will not usually be the finest forms; plants which are divisions of named varieties will be the most choice but also the most expensive. Inferior seedlings are sometimes sold as named varieties so if possible see the plants in flower first.

Cultivation

It is not fussy as to soil, although not happy in waterlogged conditions, and prefers at least a little shade though often flowers earlier in the sun. A regular spring mulch with organic matter will help keep the plants thriving. Leaf spot may be a problem with this plant. Regular spraying with a fungicide containing prapiconazole (e.g. Murphy Tumbleblite) should solve the problem.

Propagation

If you really insist on propagating, plants can be divided in spring after flowering, but they most certainly make better plants if simply left alone.

Uses in the garden

This is definitely a front-of-the-border plant and is at its best in a raised bed, so that it's easier to see the nodding flowers. It is also good in drifts between later-flowering shrubs.

Alternatives

One of the best alternatives to the normal white, and one that's fairly easy to find, is 'Guttatus' which is heavily spotted with purple inside. An excellent range of other forms is available from specialists but there may be a waiting list.

Lobelia
'Bees Flame'

Striking flowers and foliage
Half-hardy, to 4ft (1.2m)

PROBABLY A hybrid between the dark-leaved *L. fulgens* and the green-leaved *L. cardinalis*, this tall, upright plant reaches about 4ft (1.2m) and has deep beetroot-red foliage. The rich scarlet flowers overtop the foliage in a tall spike from mid summer onwards. Each flower has a large showy lower lip.

Cultivation

It thrives best in fertile, moist soil in a sunny situation. In my garden, a well-drained soil in a sunless (but not overhung) border also seems to suit it well.

This and other similar varieties are often reckoned to be slightly tender but in fact it's

The beetroot-red foliage and scarlet flowers of Lobelia *'Bees Flame' provide dramatic colour for the waterside, or a border with moist soil.*

not as simple as that. It seems to be mild wet winters that they dislike; perhaps the soft growth they make in mild conditions is susceptible to rot brought on by the damp. In my gravelly soil this variety has survived happily for three or four years in spite of some fierce winters. Slugs are a problem when, in spring, they rasp the red foliage, leaving straw-coloured patches.

Propagation

Plants can be carefully divided in spring, or leaf bud cuttings can be taken from the stems at the time of flowering. A leaf bud cutting consists of two leaves and the length of stem in between. Pinch off the lower leaf, make a clean cut below the leaf joint and make a clean cut above the other leaf. Insert the cuttings in a cuttings compost in a propagator and pot up when they have rooted. Keep them in a cold greenhouse over the winter and plant out in spring.

Uses in the garden

Occasionally used for summer bedding – rarely successfully unless the clumps are fat ones – it's often planted by the waterside amongst hostas, bog primulas and *Iris sibirica*. Here it brings some dramatic colour to the area at a time when other plants are past their best. Bog conditions are not necessary, however, and in the red border at Hidcote these dark-leaved, red-flowered varieties associate well with hot orange dahlias and cannas. They also look good surrounded by anything with finely cut, fresh green leaves, like ferns.

Alternatives

'Queen Victoria' is a similar variety and *L. fulgens* is sometimes seen.

Lupinus
'New Generation Series'

Robust cottage-garden
perennial
Hardy, to 4–5ft (1.2–1.5m)

THIS STRAIN was introduced quite recently by Woodfield Brothers, who spent many years developing them. They are tall – 4–5ft (1.2–1.5m) – and come in an extraordinary range of colours. They are a great improvement on the old Russell varieties which have deteriorated in recent years. Apart from the excellent range of colours from brick red, through pinks, lemons and white together with bicolours, they have one very useful characteristic. The flowers at the bottom of the spike don't fade and wither before the flowers at the top of the spike are open. This greatly enhances the quality of the display in the garden. They also seem to be especially strong stemmed, so may not need staking.

Cultivation

A well-drained but fertile soil in full sun suits them best though they are very adaptable plants and will be happy in most soils if they are improved before planting. However, full sun really is essential for the best plants. After flowering, cut back the stems and foliage hard and even if you get no more flowers you will stimulate an attractive mound of foliage. If the weather is dry immediately after this treatment, water well. Mildew can be a problem after flowering and I've also found the huge, grey, lupin aphid very troublesome.

Propagation

Seed of the 'New Generation' strain is available from the raisers; seed saved from your own plants will give good but unpredictable results. Sow in spring or summer for flowering the following year. Cuttings can be rooted in the same way as delphiniums, and plants can be split, with great care.

Uses in the garden

These lupins are so floriferous that they can be rather overpowering for cottage-style gardens and mixed borders if used in large groups. A clump of three makes a powerful focal point when in flower. They make wonderful cut flowers but must be kept upright between cutting and arranging, for if laid flat, the tips will curl upwards.

Alternatives

There are so many colours in this range that you won't need to look elsewhere unless you need a dwarf type, in which case, try the 'Gallery' strain.

Kniphofia
'Little Maid'

Smaller-than-average
red-hot poker
Hardy, to 2ft (60cm)

THIS IS one of a number of pokers raised and introduced by nurserywoman Beth Chatto in the 1970s. It is a dwarf form, reaching only 2ft (60cm) in height at most and often only 18in (45cm). The slightly arching foliage is narrow and, in autumn, the sleek flower spikes arise from the centre of each tuft, the flowers lining about half the stem. The buds are green and open to ivory white.

Cultivation

This tolerant plant, given full sun and good drainage, is not difficult to please.

Propagation

The clumps, which increase steadily, can be easily divided in spring.

Uses in the garden

'Little Maid' is a fine front-of-the-border plant: the narrow leaves look good while it's not flowering and it's attractive set amongst bronze leaves such as those of *Heuchera* 'Palace Purple', which the flowers overtop conveniently.

Alternatives

Other Beth Chatto varieties are the much taller but wonderfully coloured 'Green Jade' and 'Strawberries and Cream', with pink-flushed buds opening to cream flowers.

HERBS

THE SCENT and the flavour of herbs make them essential plants for any civilized garden – especially when it's so difficult to buy a good range of really fresh herbs in the shops. Taking a few steps down the path and cutting just what you need moments before you use it ensures that you get the best possible flavour from the plant.

As well as selecting herbs for their usefulness in the kitchen I've also had in mind their value as garden plants. For it always seems to me that if we're to grow herbs then we should choose varieties that look good in the garden. And it has to be said that the plain green foliage of many herbs is not exciting.

Fortunately many herbs come in forms with coloured or variegated leaves and these make a valuable contribution to ornamental borders and container plantings. They can be planted with the shrubs and perennials and not look out of place but if you choose instead to group them all together into a herb garden, it will certainly be a colourful one.

Ocimum basilicum
'Dark Opal'

Purple basil
Half-hardy annual, to 18in
(45cm)

Basil (Ocimum basilicum) *needs a warm, sunny spot in the garden. The purple-leaved form, 'Dark Purple', associates well with geraniums.*

A VARIETY of the plain green-leaved basil grows naturally in India and was brought to Britain in about 1548. 'Dark Opal' is a half-hardy annual herb reaching about 18in (45cm) in height, with large, slightly floppy oval leaves up to 3in (7.5cm) long. In this variety they are a shining dark purple shade. In late summer the stems are topped with pink flowers.

Cultivation

Basil likes a warm sheltered spot in plenty of sunshine and a soil that is rich but well drained. Plant out after the last frosts.

Propagation

Sow the seeds in threes in small pots in a heated propagator in spring and after germination remove the two weakest seedlings. Grow on fairly warm before planting out.

Uses in the garden

The shining purple colour looks good with scarlet or white flowers.

Uses in the kitchen

Basil's strong, pungent flavour is always associated with tomato recipes including pizzas, pasta and rice dishes.

Alternatives

The plain green-leaved version is less attractive but just as good for the kitchen.

Thymus × citriodorus
'Variegatus'

Variegated thyme
Hardy shrub, to 9in (23cm)

THIS IS a variegated version of the hybrid between the common bushy thyme, *Thymus vulgaris*, and the creeping thyme, *T. serpyllum*. It is a neat, erect-growing but well branched shrublet reaching little more than 9in (23cm) in

height. The young stems are dark pink. The flowers, which appear in early summer at the tip of the shoots, are also pink and the greyish green leaves, very prettily edged with white, complete this attractive colour combination. The leaves are scented with lemon.

Cultivation

Again, a well-drained sunny site is necessary and this plant also thrives in a trough or large pot. Make sure plants are not over-shadowed by larger neighbours or they will lose their leaves and die. Trim the plants after flowering to keep them well furnished with foliage.

Propagation

Cuttings root fairly easily in a sandy compost in mid summer.

Uses in the garden

Variegated thyme is best in a raised bed, trough or large pot where the drainage is good and the plant won't be smothered.

Uses in the kitchen

The thyme flavour with its overlay of lemon makes this plant an interesting variation on the ordinary thyme for flavouring stuffings, cottage cheese, meats and salads.

Alternatives

There are other variegated thymes although the names are rather confused. 'Silver Posie' is a name often attached to this plant but also to variegated versions of the common thyme. If in doubt, look at them, sniff the leaves and then decide what to buy.

Monarda didyma
'Cambridge Scarlet'

Bergamot
Hardy perennial, to 2ft (60cm)

THE SPECIES grows wild in North America and the better coloured 'Cambridge Scarlet' has been grown since at least 1913. It is a well-known herbaceous perennial plant, reaching about 2ft (60cm) in height, with a steadily creeping rootstock. The oval leaves are dark in colour and carried on stiff stems that terminate in flowering spikes carrying dense tiers of hooked, bright scarlet flowers in summer and early autumn.

Cultivation

Bergamot prefers a rich, moist soil and is even perfectly happy on stream sides and at the edges of ponds. It's also happier in some shade, otherwise it tends to lose its lower leaves. It dislikes being overshadowed by other plants. In hot summers and dry soils mildew can be a problem, so plant in the right place.

Propagation

Bergamot is easily increased by division and, indeed, it likes being divided regularly, every year if growing well. Otherwise it can become very bare at the centre and produce poor foliage and flowers.

Uses in the garden

A long-time favourite for herbaceous borders, its bright flowers always enliven herb gardens. After flowering it looks less than elegant and is best cut down low.

Uses in the kitchen

Bergamot is used to make a soothing tea that also settles the stomach. It is also used to flavour some China teas, and was used in America as a substitute for Indian tea.

The aromatic leaves of bergamot (Monarda didyma) *are topped with showy flowers.*

Chives (Allium schoenoprasum) produce masses of attractive ball-shaped heads of lilac pink flowers in summer.

and cutting back hard into old wood gives unpredictable results – the most likely being death. Cuttings root easily so after a few years older plants can be dug up and young plants set in their place.

Propagation

Tip cuttings root fairly easily at any time from mid spring to mid autumn if set in a well-drained cuttings compost in a warm propagator. Shoots lying on the soil tend to root into it and can be detached and replanted. Unfortunately they sometimes make lopsided plants.

Uses in the garden

A good front-of-the-border plant to spill out on to paving, it looks well with limy-yellow-flowered *Alchemilla mollis* and silver foliage such as artemisias. In the herb garden, golden marjoram and various coloured-leaved thymes are good neighbours.

Uses in the kitchen

Sage is traditionally used in stuffings and sauces for game and rich meat. Small quantities can be used in salads, and cheeses flavoured with sage are becoming increasingly popular.

Alternatives

There are other coloured-leaved varieties. 'Purpurascens Variegata' is purple with occasional white streaks; 'Icterina' is grey green, variegated with yellow; 'Tricolor' has leaves patterned in green, pink and white; 'Kew Gold' is uniformly yellow; 'Aurea' usually turns out to be 'Icterina'. They're all worth growing.

Alternatives

There are varieties in other colours. 'Croftway Pink' and the deep purple 'Prairie Night' are worth trying but seedlings often produce flowers in rather watery shades.

Salvia officinalis
'Purpurascens'

Purple sage

Hardy shrub, to 18in (45cm)

THIS IS a variety of the sage that grows wild in the Mediterranean. It is a spreading shrub, making a plant up to 3ft (90cm) across and only half as high with long, elliptical foliage. These long-stemmed leaves are a lovely dusky purple, darkest when young and with a rough veiny texture. In early summer mature plants produce spikes of dark purplish blue flowers which go very well with the foliage.

Cultivation

Like so many herbs, it prefers a sunny well-drained site. In wetter conditions or in heavier soil it may be damaged in winter.

Trim back towards the base of the current season's wood after flowering. Plants often become straggly and very bare in the centre

Allium schoenoprasum

Chives

Hardy perennial, to 12in (30cm)

THIS PLANT grows wild all over the Northern Hemisphere and is one of the most familiar of all herbs. The clumps of long, dark green tubular leaves have a delicate, subtle, oniony flavour. They reach about 12in (30cm) in height and in summer rounded heads of lilac-pink flowers appear.

Cultivation

Chives will grow in most soils and situations

but thrive most heartily in rich, moist but well-drained soil in full sun. As they can be cut continually from early spring to late autumn they need a good soil to promote constant regrowth. For cutting, especially early and late, plants can be potted up and moved into the conservatory or green-house in autumn.

Propagation

Clumps can be divided and replanted in spring and autumn.

Uses in the garden

A good edging to a path, chives can also be used with broad-leaved plants such as hostas or bergenias and are good in dense mixed planting where their leaves and flowers flop out amongst other plants. They thrive in pots of soil-based compost if watered and fed regularly.

Uses in the kitchen

Fresh leaves (cut up into small pieces with kitchen scissors) can be mixed with cottage cheese, sprinkled on soups and added to omelettes. Salads of all sorts benefit from a few chives – both the leaves and the flowers.

Alternatives

'Forescate' produces more flowers than the standard variety.

Borago officinalis
Borage
Hardy annual, to 18in (45cm)

THIS RATHER rough and hairy annual grows wild in the Mediterranean. It reaches about 18in (45cm) in height and branches well if given the space to do so. The star-shaped flowers, which appear for many weeks from mid summer from a spring sowing, are about 1in (2.5cm) across, sharp blue in colour and are produced in uncurling heads, rather like for-get-me-nots. Old plants can look rather rough and scraggy.

Cultivation

A sunny site and well-drained soil suits bor-age best. It will also thrive in moist soils that are not waterlogged and in partial shade, but the plants may become drawn and floppy in such situations. Seeds from the first flowers often drop, germinate and then flower in late autumn of the same year.

Propagation

Sow the seed outside where it is to flower in early spring and thin the seedlings first to about 3in (7.5cm), then to 9–12in (23–30cm) apart.

Uses in the garden

A fine plant for the annual border, it looks good in a broad group but one or two speci-mens are welcome in any sunny place.

Uses in the kitchen

The rather juicy leaves have a cucumber-like flavour and are used in fruit cups and summer punches. They are also good in salads. Borage has a slightly salty flavour and so is sometimes used as a seasoning for low-salt diets. The candied flowers are used as cake decorations.

Alternatives

There are none.

Borage (Borago officinalis) *has a long flowering season, striking large leaves and pretty blue flowers.*

Foeniculum vulgare
'Purpureum'

Bronze fennel
Hardy perennial, 4–5ft
(1.2–1.5m)

FENNEL ORIGINALLY grew wild in the Mediterranean region but has now spread to many other areas. It is a tall and upright hardy perennial reaching 4–5ft (1.2–1.5m) in height. The leaves are very finely cut into narrow threads and are a very attractive deep purplish-bronze. In mid to late summer the stems are topped with flat heads of tiny yellowish-green flowers.

Cultivation

A sunny site in well-drained soil will produce the best plants, but as long as the soil is not waterlogged and the shade not too dense, you should have reasonable results. On heavy soils in wet winters the crown may rot but improving the soil with grit or compost when planting will help. If you prefer to restrict the plant to a mound of delicate foliage, the flower stems can be cut out but this is a determined plant and it will keep trying to flower. It's usually stout enough not to demand staking. Unless you want some seed, cut the flower stems down after flowering, and water and feed well to create a foaming mound of brown foliage.

Propagation

Division can be risky as the roots often rot from the cut surfaces but if you allow a stem to set seed this can be collected and sown, or allowed to fall and germinate.

Uses in the garden

A fine plant in spring with white tulips; later in the season it associates well with rusty rudbeckias, fiery crocosmias and yellow, orange or white lilies. It makes a good focal point in the herb garden.

Uses in the kitchen

Fennel is traditionally used with fish, which can be baked on a bed of fennel shoots – fresh or dried – or stuffed with fennel leaves. Alternatively it can be used to make a sauce. Chewing fennel seeds is said to stave off hunger.

Alternatives

The plain green-leaved fennel is itself a very attractive plant that is well-worth growing. Other dark-leaved forms with names like 'Black Form', 'Giant Bronze' and 'Smoky' are all much the same as 'Purpureum'.

Rosmarinus
'Miss Jessopp's Upright'

Rosemary
Half-hardy shrub, to 6ft (1.8m)

THE ORIGINAL species, *Rosmarinus officinalis*, grows wild in the Mediterranean where its scent adds to the fragrance of the maquis. This variety and a number of others are selections from wild populations. It is a rather upright evergreen shrub with upward-sweeping branches. These are clothed in long, narrow, dusky green foliage that gives off the familiar aroma when bruised or crushed, or on hot sultry days. The flowers are soft blue and can appear early in spring and intermittently until late summer.

Cultivation

A well-drained site, preferably with an alkaline soil and full sun, suits it best. If grown as a hedge, a couple of horizontal wires will

Rosmarinus officinalis 'Miss Jessopp's Upright' is an upright variety of rosemary with profuse soft-blue flowers.

help keep it in order. In colder areas this and other varieties are sometimes damaged or even killed in bad winters. The weight of snow also breaks the branches of this variety in particular and it pays to knock snow off regularly.

Tidy up the plants by pruning after any winter damage and at the same time improve the shape by cutting back inelegant branches to good side shoots.

Uses in the garden

'Miss Jessop's Upright' is good as an informal hedge, a specimen plant in a dry, sunny border and in cooler areas is a first-rate plant for a large tub; it can then be moved to a sheltered spot, a conservatory or a greenhouse for the winter. Its striking shape makes it a wonderful winter feature in an otherwise rather bare herb garden.

Uses in the kitchen

A classic herb for lamb dishes, it's also popular for barbecues; twigs thrown on the charcoal scent both the air and the food. Rosemary also deepens the colour of hair if used as a rinse.

Alternatives

There is a number of other good rosemaries to choose from: 'Severn Sea' is very dark blue, 'Majorca' has pink flowers and a drooping habit and the splendid *R. lavandulaceus* is a rather tender trailer with noticeably short leaves.

Lavandula
'Hidcote'

Lavender

Hardy perennial, to 18in (45cm)

A VARIETY of *Lavandula angustifolia*, 'Hidcote' is thought to have been brought from France by Lawrence Johnston and planted at his garden at Hidcote Manor. It gained an RHS Award of Merit in 1950 and a First Class certificate in 1963. It is a compact evergreen reaching about 18in (45cm) in height and as much across, with narrow grey-green leaves. The flowers, which appear in fat spikes all summer, are a deep violet-purple. A few flowers may also appear nearer the base of the flower stem, some way below the main spike. The fragrance is too familiar to need description.

Lavandula *'Hidcote' is a must for any garden. The deep violet-blue fragrant flowers are a great draw for bees.*

Cultivation

A bright sunny position in a well-drained though not necessarily sandy soil is essential. Neutral or alkaline conditions are preferable but otherwise 'Hidcote' is not fussy.

Plants are best trimmed back regularly each spring and dead-headed after flowering. Old straggly plants can usually be rejuvenated by cutting them back very hard in spring and ensuring that they're well watered if the spring is a dry one and fed with a liquid feed.

Uses in the garden

'Hidcote' is excellent as a low hedge round beds of shrub roses, as an edging for mixed borders, along paths or in the vegetable garden. It also makes a fine, neat, container plant.

Uses in the kitchen

It is occasionally used with strongly-flavoured meats like venison but more often in *pot-pourri*, as an astringent for the skin, or to scent bedding and so on.

Alternatives

'Hidcote Giant' is altogether taller and more coarse, but is also more fragrant. 'Hidcote Pink' is similar to 'Hidcote' apart from the flower colour. 'Vera' (Dutch lavender) has paler flowers, greyer foliage and is taller than 'Hidcote'.

Melissa officinalis
'All Gold'

Golden lemon balm
Hardy perennial, 18–24in
(45–60cm)

THIS STRONGLY lemon-scented hardy perennial originated from the Middle East but is now naturalized in Europe. It reaches about 18–24in (45–60cm) in height with upright, branching growth. The neat lobed leaves have a very strong lemon flavour. The flowers, which appear from mid summer to early autumn, are white and insignificant.

Cultivation

It is best planted in a fairly fertile soil that is not too dry and in a site that will give at least partial shade. The full shade of a cool wall will ensure that the leaves are not scorched.

Propagation

The clumps will spread steadily and can easily be divided and replanted in spring and autumn whenever necessary. If allowed to flower and set seed, golden lemon balm will produce seedlings around the garden. Unfortunately these will quite probably turn out to be much more vigorous green-leaved plants.

Uses in the garden

A fine plant for enlivening darker parts of the garden which are not too dry. Although it makes an attractive rounded hummock when young, it stretches up later so must be placed accordingly. It looks lovely with bronze fennel.

Uses in the kitchen

Splendidly lemony in summer drinks without being too acid and the fresh leaves are also good as a tea. Use it in salads too or instead of shredded lemon peel.

Alternatives

The green-leaved plant has the same flavour and is an attractive plant. There is also a variety with yellow-speckled leaves, usually known as 'Aureum', although plants with entirely yellow leaves are sometimes sold under this name.

Origanum vulgare
'Aureum'

Golden marjoram
Hardy perennial, to 12in
(30cm)

THIS HERBACEOUS perennial herb is a yellow-leaved variety of the wild marjoram, or oregano, which grows on chalky and limestone soils in Britain and southern Europe. The dark stems carry small leaves which start off bright butter-yellow in spring but eventually fade towards green later in the year. The flowers, which appear from mid summer to mid autumn, are rosy purple and very popular with bees. The plants tend to spread.

Cultivation

Golden marjoram seems to thrive in many situations but a hot dry site with good drainage produces the most compact plants with the best flavour. Unfortunately, in hot summers it suffers from leaf scorch which results in a rather scrappy-looking plant. I refuse to compromise and grow it in full sun, but shade at midday would help. As the flower stems elongate, cut it back very hard

Lemon balm (Melissa officinalis) is an attractive clump-forming plant, but is inclined to reproduce itself rapidly. 'All Gold' is an attractive golden-leaved variety.

and, if not short of water, shoots should grow again quickly making a fresher mat of limy yellow. This will also encourage it to spread although it can be confined to its space by forking out unwanted extremities.

Propagation

Many shoots produce roots at the base and it's a simple matter to detach some and replant them elsewhere.

Uses in the garden

Golden marjoram makes a good front-of-the-border plant with grasses and hostas, dark-leaved sedums and potentillas. In the herb garden leave the flowers on to attract bees and butterflies.

Uses in the kitchen

Use sparingly with sautéd vegetables, tomato dishes, meats and soups and in stuffings for poultry and game.

Alternatives

There are other ornamental marjorams including a white-flowered version of this yellow-leaved variety, 'Aureum Album', and a yellow, crinkly-leaved one, 'Aureum Crispum'; 'Gold Tip' has gold tips to the leaves that fade as they age and 'Tracy's Yellow Form' is said never to fade or scorch but is very difficult to find.

Petroselinum crispum
'Bravour'

Curled parsley
Hardy annual, to 12in (30cm)

Parsley is too well known to demand description. 'Bravour' is a modern variety of a species that probably originated in the west Mediterranean region. It is especially crisped and curled and a rich, deep emerald-green colour. It makes rounded mounds of foliage, renews itself constantly all summer and is very resistant to bolting.

Cultivation

Grow it in sun or partial shade in any reasonably fertile soil.

Propagation

Sow seed in spring in a heated propagator or outside in short rows. The seed is un-usually slow to germinate so don't lose patience if nothing appears for three or four weeks. Outside, sow a few radish seeds in the row with the parsley. These germinate quickly and mark the row so it's easy to hoe on either side.

Uses in the garden

It makes a good temporary edging or ground cover plant to offset other plants, especially those with bright yellow or orange flowers. It tones down marigolds well. Grow it in large numbers for not only is it invaluable in the kitchen, but it's the ideal temporary ground cover and filler in beds and borders.

Uses in the kitchen

Parsley is the universal herb for garnishes and flavouring. It is good in a sauce for white fish, with egg dishes, in and on soup,

Golden marjoram (Origanum vulgare 'Aureum') is a yellow-leaved variety of wild marjoram that makes an excellent border-edging plant.

in stuffings and sausages and with meats of all sorts. As one cook put it, 'If in doubt, fling in some parsley'.

Alternatives

There are a number of other crisply curled varieties such as 'Curlina' and 'Moss Curled'. The plain-leaved 'French' is said to have the best flavour and 'Par-Cel' looks like parsley but tastes of celery.

Hyssopus officinalis

Hyssop
Hardy perennial, to 18in
(45cm)

THIS NEAT shrubby plant, which grows in southern Europe, has a dense, bushy habit and reaches about 18in (45cm) in height. The leaves are long and narrow and the flowers are usually blue and not very large, but grow in attractive, compact, rather one-sided spikes at the tips of the shoots from mid summer until well into the autumn.

Cultivation

Like many herbs, hyssop prefers a sunny site and a light soil but is reasonably tolerant of other soils except those that are waterlogged. Hyssop can suffer in bad winters so overwinter a few cuttings in a cold greenhouse. Clip over in spring to encourage dense rather than straggly growth. If plenty of shoots are removed for cooking this usually keeps the plants bushy.

Propagation

Hyssop can be raised from seed, but tip cuttings about 3in (7.5cm) long, taken before flowering or from non-flowering side shoots, will root easily from late spring onwards.

Uses in the garden

Hyssop makes a pretty, informal low hedge in the herb garden or a delightful edging to a cottage garden path.

Uses in the kitchen

The flavour is slightly bitter and minty and a few young tips can be chopped into salads. It is often recommended to help the digestion of fatty meats and with strongly flavoured game. Hyssop is also used to make Chartreuse and to flavour sausages.

Alternatives

There are very attractive white- and pink-flowered varieties, which look well planted with the species.

Mentha suaveolens
'Variegata'

Variegated apple mint
Hardy perennial, 18–24in
(45–60cm)

THIS VARIEGATED version of the apple mint is a moderately invasive mint with rather woolly, apple-green foliage edged with pure white. The shoots reach only about 18–24in (45–60cm) in height and spread less vigorously than most mints. Growth is not quick and for some time the foliage is neat and pretty, stretching out and becoming rather floppy late in the season. Pure white shoots may appear.

Cultivation

It thrives best in a reasonably fertile soil in at least partial shade; full sun may cause the white leaf edges to scorch.

Propagation

It is easily increased either by lifting the whole plant and splitting and replanting it, or by detaching rooted shoots.

Uses in the garden

It's not necessary to confine this plant as one does with other mints. It looks wonderful with purple bugle and blue-leaved hostas, and provides an attractive contrast with the deep green of box hedges in a formal herb garden.

Uses in the kitchen

The flavour of this mint is decidedly fruity. It is also known as pineapple mint though it has no scent of pineapples whatsoever. I've used it with new potatoes in the usual way, and as an unusual addition to salads.

Alternatives

The only other variegated mint worth considering is the charming variegated ginger mint, Mentha × gentilis 'Variegata'. A neater plant, it reaches only about 12–15in (30–38cm). The leaves are splashed with bright yellow and the flavour is spicy, rather than specifically gingery.

CONNOISSEURS' PLANTS

IN THIS FINAL chapter of my survey of the very best of all garden plants I have selected plants that simply have great intrinsic merit. These are less recognized, less widely available plants that deserve to be grown more often. Some plants are difficult to propagate and so nurseries find it hard to produce them in large quantities. Others may simply be difficult to grow without special care. Good plants are sometimes ignored because similar, but not necessarily better varieties are more effectively publicized. And of course, plants can be uncommon because they're relatively new; others may simply be unappreciated.

In choosing these special, connoisseurs' plants I've broken my own rules as some of them are a little less easy to grow than the other plants I've featured and may need just a little special care and attention. Some are also less easily obtainable from garden centres and nurseries but none are entirely impossible to get hold of, though there may only be one or two places that stock them.

The whole point about these plants is that they're worth the extra little bit of trouble to grow or to find. They're the plants that visitors greet with surprise and delight, those unique plants that give special pleasure when they thrive and which make a garden chic.

Euphorbia
'Lambrook Yellow'

Eye-catching front-of-border plant

Hardy perennial, to 3ft (90cm)

THIS VARIETY arose as a chance seedling in Margery Fish's garden at East Lambrook Manor in the early 1960s, and is sometimes known as 'Lambrook Gold'. It is a rather shrubby-looking perennial reaching about 3ft (90cm) in height but often rather more across. The stout stems, which all arise from around ground level, are lined with narrow, dark, greyish green leaves and topped for several spring months with cylindrical heads of almost buttery yellow flowers. After flowering the shoots die, or should be cut out, and new shoots grow from the base to flower the following year.

Cultivation

It is happy in most well-drained soils but definitely not in heavy clay where it will tend to suffer in even average winters. Very hard winters can kill the plant, especially on wet soils, and heavy snow can damage the branches. Full sun is definitely preferable. Shoots should be removed once they have flowered, leaving the young shoots to grow on to flower the following year.

Propagation

Cuttings of short shoots can be taken whenever you can find them during the season and rooted in a heated propagator. Milky latex oozes from the cut stems and you should be sure to keep this away from your eyes. Dipping the cut ends in hormone rooting powder not only helps dry up the sap but also aids rooting. Do not expect a high percentage take.

Although difficult to root from cuttings, this is the only way to ensure that the true form is perpetuated. Margery Fish herself said 'most of its seedlings resemble the parent plant', but this cannot be guaranteed.

Uses in the garden

A dramatic architectural plant, it is instantly recognizable by its growth habit and its clouds of buttery flowers. At the front of a border, where it can slightly overhang the path, it is very effective.

There are many species and varieties of euphorbia. This one, 'Lambrook Yellow', arose as a chance seedling in Margery Fish's garden in the early 1960s. A shrubby perennial, it is topped with butter-yellow heads of flowers throughout the spring.

Alternatives

Two forms that are encountered more often are also well worth growing. *E. characias* is around the height of 'Lambrook Yellow' but has greenish flowers with a chocolate eye and *E. characias* subspecies *wulfenii* can reach up to 6ft (1.8m). It also has green flowers, but with a green eye.

Berberis × lologensis
'Apricot Queen'

Evergreen back-of-border plant
Hardy shrub, to 10ft (3m)

THIS IS A hybrid between the familiar *B. darwinii* and the less common *B. linearifolia*. Both grow wild near Lake Lolog in Argentina where natural hybrids occur – hence the name – and where this was discovered in 1927. It is an evergreen shrub of upright habit eventually reaching 10ft (3m) but taking many years to do so. The small, glossy, holly-like leaves are dark green with silvery undersides and very similar to those of *Berberis darwinii*. The apricot flowers are larger than those of most berberis and line the older branches in late spring. They're followed in autumn by blue berries, darkening to black.

Cultivation

It is happy in most soils except chalky or very dry ones, but can be damaged by icy winds. It grows best in light shade or full sun. It can be rather slow to establish and plenty of organic matter in the preparation of the site will help. No pruning is required, except for occasional tidying.

Propagation

Short cuttings with a heel of older wood can be taken in autumn and set in well-drained soil in a cold frame and should be ready to move a year later.

Uses in the garden

A splendid back-of-the-border plant, it will need protection from encroaching perennials as it grows if it is to retain its shape.

Alternatives

B. darwinii is an old favourite and often planted but the larger-flowered *B. lineari-folia*, especially the variety 'Orange King', is a good alternative.

Euonymus alatus

Autumn-tinted foliage plant
Hardy shrub, to 6ft (1.8m)

FOUND GROWING wild in China and Japan, this widely spreading deciduous shrub is grown for its stunning autumn colour. Although starting off as a more or less rounded plant, it spreads increasingly as it gets older, eventually reaching 6ft (1.8m) in height and twice as much across. The leaves are oval and greyish green until autumn when they turn an astonishing scarlet shade with a slight pinkish tinge. The squarish stems are also distinctive, having four slightly corky flanges running along their length.

Cultivation

It is very tolerant of soil types although it's sometimes said that richer soil increases the size of the corky wings. Full sun produces the best autumn colour. Pruning is not usually required.

Propagation

Peg down the lower branches in autumn to encourage them to root or sow seeds in a warm greenhouse in spring.

Uses in the garden

It is best as a single specimen or in a group; its spreading habit makes it difficult to fit into a border.

The foliage of Euonymus alatus *turns an arresting brilliant scarlet in autumn and, for this reason alone, the shrub is worth growing as a specimen plant.*

The glamorous, scented spring flowers of the tree paeony, Paeonia suffruticosa *'Joseph Rock' are nearly 6in (15cm) across. Unfortunately, they are susceptible to spring frost, so shelter is essential.*

Alternatives

The variety 'Compactus' is occasionally seen and is, of course, more compact. *E. phellomanus* has similar winged shoots and its relative lack of autumn colour is balanced by the of showy pink fruits.

Paeonia suffruticosa
'Joseph Rock'

Tree paeony

Hardy shrub, to 6ft (1.8m)

THIS TREE paeony was found in the Kansu province of China by Reginald Farrer but seed was first sent back by the American, Joseph Rock, to various British gardeners. It makes a branching shrub of slightly lax habit eventually reaching about 6ft (1.8m) in height – though it may take 50 years to do so. In late spring the stupendous flowers appear; they are about 6in (15cm) or more across. The plant collector

Reginald Farrer, the first European to see this plant in China, described the flower as 'that single enormous blossom, waved and crimped into the boldest grace of line, of absolutely pure white, with feathering of deepest maroon radiating at the base of the petals from the boss of golden fluff at the flower's heart'. The flowers are exquisitely scented too: according to Mr Farrer, 'the breath of them went out upon the twilight as sweet as any rose'.

Cultivation

At Highdown in Sussex it grows in an exposed place on pure chalk; at Kew in a more sheltered spot on light silt. Protection from early frost is essential as many tree paeonies have soft new growth which is very easily damaged by early frosts. They start to shoot early and so are very susceptible.

Some gardeners erect a protective cover of hessian, or nylon or plastic net to prevent damage. Siting so that the new shoots are not struck by the early morning sun in spring is a wise precaution. No pruning is usually necessary.

Propagation

This plant is virtually impossible to propagate. Seeds occasionally germinate but may not come true; cuttings may occasionally root; layers may occasionally be successful. Few gardeners will want to risk lifting a plant to divide it. The result is that it is virtually impossible to buy. It's worth asking shrub specialists, if only to keep them aware of how much demand there is but I cannot guarantee that you will ever find one.

Uses in the garden

Plant it where it will amaze visitors.

Alternatives

There are many other tree paeonies that are easier to find in nurseries, including doubles in brilliant colours, but none quite like this one. If you can't find 'Joseph Rock' go for simple *P. suffruticosa*.

Codonopsis convolvulacea

Delicate blue-flowered twiner
Hardy, to 6ft (1.8m)

THIS TUBEROUS climber grows wild in the Himalayas. It has slender, twining stems reaching 6ft (1.8m) in height when happy but usually rather less. In early and mid summer the large, soft blue, nodding flowers appear and open widely, almost making a five-pointed star.

Cultivation

It grows in any well-drained soil that is not parched and is equally happy in a peat garden with good drainage or a sunny border with a fair amount of organic matter.

Propagation

Sow seed as soon as it's ripe or the following spring in a peat-based seed compost and leave outside.

Uses in the garden

Although this plant is a twining climber, it is not satisfactory grown up trellis or netting. It will look much more natural planted at the base of a rhododendron or other shrub through which it can scramble.

Alternatives

I find the bell-shaped flowers of *C. clematidea* prettier – white with a tint of soft blue with purple and yellow rings inside – but the plant is altogether coarser and the leaves have a rather unpleasant smell.

Cheiranthus
'Harpur Crewe'

Old-fashioned cottage
wallflower
Hardy shrub, to 18in (45cm)

NAMED AFTER the Rev Edward Harpur Crewe, a mid-Victorian cleric, this plant was apparently known from the early 17th century. It is an old-fashioned cottage wallflower that makes a bushy dense-growing shrub of rounded habit, reaching about 15–18 in (38–45cm) in height with short, rather stiff green leaves. The flower spikes appear in spring and early summer and are packed with sweetly scented, fully double, bright yellow flowers a little smaller than those of the more familiar bedding types. 'Harpur Crewe' tends to be a short-lived plant and may suddenly die while in an apparently healthy state after just a few years.

The old-fashioned cottage wallflower, Cheiranthus 'Harpur Crewe' makes a bushy shrub with highly scented double yellow flowers.

Cultivation

A sunny site in well-drained soil is ideal though it will tolerate heavier soil that has been improved. Shelter it from high winds to prevent loosening of the roots which can cause premature death. No pruning, save dead heading, is usually necessary.

Propagation

Short cuttings 2–3in (5–7.5cm) long can be taken in summer and early autumn and rooted in a well-drained compost in a heated propagator. This variety will never produce any seed.

Uses in the garden

It is a good plant for the corner of a raised bed and for the sunnier parts of the cottage garden. Plant it where you can appreciate the scent.

Alternatives

Similar varieties include 'Chevithorne', which is said to be a little shorter, 'Baden Powell' and 'Miss Massey'.

Lapageria rosea

Exquisite bell-shaped flowers
Tender climber, to 12ft (3.6m)

THIS SLIGHTLY tender, twining climber grows wild in Argentina and Chile. It can reach 12 ft (3.6m) but often grows to no more than half as much. The leaves are very leathery, rather like those of a hoya, and are carried on slender woody stems. The pendulous flowers are about 3in (7.5cm) long with six wavy petals in deep red – or occasionally pink or white. They appear from early summer and will continue until early autumn.

Cultivation

This is a fussy plant requiring a warm, sheltered but shady wall – a difficult combination. A place on a warm wall shaded by a tree or evergreen shrubs is probably ideal. Although often thought to need acid conditions, a soil rich in organic matter is probably more important. As it must never dry out, mulching is sensible. Little pruning is usually required, although plants that are growing well and throwing up shoots from ground level can have any older, weak growth removed occasionally.

Propagation

Propagation is almost impossible for the home gardener, although a few people have had success with seed.

Uses in the garden

It grows best on a wall rather than through a shrub as it's warmer and is also excellent for a conservatory. Most gardeners are satisfied simply by getting this rather tender plant to thrive without wondering how it will associate with other plants.

Alternatives

There's nothing quite like it. 'Albiflora'

across, slightly ribbed and narrowing to a point; they are a penetrating misty blue colour. The flower spikes are undistinguished.

Cultivation

I've seen it thriving or grown it well myself in a wide variety of situations from improved heavy clay to gravelly loam, in full sun or under a walnut tree (though, of course, the latter was the least successful). The clumps spread steadily but can be divided every year if you want to increase them quickly. If you leave the unremarkable seed heads in place you might possibly get a few self-sown seedlings.

Propagation

Plants are easily raised from seed sown as soon as it is ripe in late summer, or in spring. Clumps can also be pulled apart in spring and the pieces replanted.

Uses in the garden

The unusual colour of this grass makes it a wonderful open carpeting for pink roses and a splendid foil for hostas and other broad-leaved plants. With dark foliage like *Lobelia* 'Queen Victoria' behind it and the ornamental beetroot 'Bull's Blood', in front, it's very impressive.

Alternatives

There are no alternatives – although there may appear to be at least one. Very similar plants, under the names of *A. magellanicum* and *A. glaucum*, are usually more spreading in habit, with flatter growth, although they usually turn out to be the more upright *A. pubiflorum*.

Hebe *'Fairfieldii'* needs a warm, sunny and sheltered spot in the garden where it will make an ideal front-of-the-border plant.

(white) and 'Nash Court' (soft pink) are very attractive forms.

Agropyron pubiflorum

Excellent carpeting plant
Hardy grass, to 18in (45cm)

THIS LESS rampant relative of couch grass, *A. repens*, grows wild in Tasmania and was introduced to the UK in the last few years. It is a clump-forming grass and reaches about 18in (45cm) in height, with rather loose arching growth. The narrow leaves are about ¼in (6mm)

Hebe
'Fairfieldii'

Another good front-of-border
shrub
Hardy shrub, to 3ft (90cm)

ACROSS BETWEEN the lovely *H. hulkeana* and the rarely seen *H. lavaudiana*, it arose on a nursery at Fairfield, near Dunedin on South Island, New Zealand. It is rather different from the familiar hebe hybrids, being more erect and well branched with purplish shoots and growing to about 3ft (90cm). The leaves are dark and leathery, each one having a wavy, reddish edge. The small, lavender-coloured

Tropaeolum tuberosum 'Ken Aslett' is too tender to be left outdoors in cold areas, and before the first frosts, the tubers should be lifted and overwintered.

flowers are carried above foliage in open heads about 9in (23cm) long giving an attractive cloud-like effect.

Cultivation

This plant demands a warm, sunny, sheltered spot with good drainage. It pays to take cuttings in late summer in case the plant is killed by a bad winter, as may happen in colder areas. Dead-heading straight after flowering encourages bushiness and also produces material for cuttings.

Propagation

Short side shoots about 3in (7.5cm) long can be rooted in late summer and overwintered in a frost-free greenhouse for planting out in the spring.

Uses in the garden

An ideal front-of-the-border plant, it will spill prettily over on to the path.

Alternatives

H. hulkeana is a good alternative and is a slightly hardier plant, less bushy and more open in habit.

Tropaeolum tuberosum
'Ken Aslett'

Tuberous nasturtium
Half-hardy climber, to 10ft
(3m)

THE SPECIES grows wild in Peru and Bolivia. The variety 'Ken Aslett' is the only form that can be relied upon to flower generously, starting relatively early and continuing into autumn. It's named after a well-known former foreman of the rock garden at Wisley. A tuberous climber, it reaches about 10ft (3m) with small, relatively delicate, fingered leaves. It supports itself by twining its leaf stalks around any available support. The flowers, which appear from mid summer to the first frosts, are carried singly on curving stems about 6in (15cm) long and are rather tubular and a brilliant mixture of orange and burnt orange. The Peruvian Indians are said to eat the tubers but I can reveal to you that they make a singularly unremarkable meal.

Cultivation

Tubers are started into growth in spring in a frost-free greenhouse and planted out after the last frost in a sunny spot with at least reasonable soil. Netting or brushwood, or a stout shrub, will provide essential support. A less solid shrub will collapse under the weight of growth. Once the foliage has been cut back by the frost, lift the tubers carefully and store them in dry peat or sand in a greenhouse which is just frost free.

Propagation

If your plant is happy you will find that for every tuber you plant in spring you will have at least ten in the autumn. Tubers may be formed very close to the surface so don't leave it too late in the year to lift them.

Uses in the garden

It is good for clothing stout spring-flowering shrubs or evergreens or for rapidly filling empty wall space in a new garden.

Alternatives

None. Don't buy the ordinary *T. tuberosum*.

Lupinus varius

Excellent container plant
Hardy annual, to 3ft (90cm)

THIS IS A stunning annual lupin that grows wild in Israel. It has a rather succulent stem, reaching about 2–3ft (60–90cm) in height, with fingered foliage, each leaflet fringed in fine silvery hairs. The flowers are carried in rings of five on an open spike up to 15in (38cm) long. They open in rich blue with a white flash that turns almost black as the flowers age.

Cultivation

A sunny fertile soil that is reasonably well drained is essential for this unusual lupin to thrive. Plant out in early summer, stake the plants well and give them plenty of light to encourage branching. Dead head promptly to encourage continuous flowering. If badly grown and allowed to become pot-bound or too crowded, plants will soon produce just a few flowers on a single stem before dying. Even well grown plants tend to die in late summer, leaving a twiggy mass of shrivelled foliage that must be removed.

Propagation

The seeds must be soaked in warm water for 24 hours otherwise they will not take in water and germinate. Any that do not swell after 24 hours should be filed and resoaked. In mid spring they can be planted singly in 3-in (7.5-cm) pots in a temperature of not less than 50°F (10°C)–70°F (21°C) is best. As soon as the first divided leaves appear they can be moved to a cooler spot and grown on. If they threaten to become pot-bound, pot them on into 5-in (12.5-cm) pots.

Uses in the garden

This lupin is excellent in large containers. It can also be planted in any sunny, well-drained border.

Alternatives

There's nothing quite like it. The Texas blue bonnet, *L. texensis*, is a lovely plant, though altogether less dramatic.

Salvia patens
'Cambridge Blue'

Summer bedding
Half-hardy perennial, to 3ft (90cm)

THE SPECIES grows wild in Mexico, but the origin of this paler form is unclear. This tuberous half-hardy perennial grows to 2–3ft (60–90cm) in height with arrowhead-shaped, slightly rough green leaves. The large hooked flowers are a lovely pure Cambridge blue and appear in open spikes throughout the summer months.

Cultivation

Being slightly tender, plants rarely survive the winter outside. They should be planted out in a sunny site in any reasonable soil after the last frost. For overwintering either lift the whole plant and store the tubers like dahlias, or take cuttings in late summer and overwinter the young plants in their pots.

Propagation

Tubers can be carefully divided in spring, and cuttings from overwintered tubers can be taken in spring . This plant also comes true from seed which can be sown in a heated propagator in early spring and pricked out into 3-in (7.5-cm) pots for planting out after hardening off.

Uses in the garden

It looks very well with *Nicotiana* 'Lime Green' or *Helichrysum petiolare* 'Limelight' in a tub or large window box. In the border it forms a lovely sea of pale blue, and is at its best with *Argyranthemum* 'Vancouver' planted alongside.

Alternatives

The wild, Oxford blue form is a very intense colour and also a fine plant.

Iris unguicularis

Winter-flowering evergreen
Hardy perennial, to 24in
(60cm)

THIS WINTER- FLOWERING iris grows wild in Algeria and was introduced into Britain in 1845. It was once known as *I. stylosa*. It has slowly spreading roots and narrow, dark green evergreen foliage that reaches about 18–24in (45–60cm) and eventually flops at the ends. It spreads slowly when happy and in mild spells from late autumn to early spring produces delicate, sweetly scented, lavender blue flowers with yellow and white marks. Slugs sometimes eat the buds, so protect them with pellets.

The handsome winter-flowering Iris unguicularis *has scented lavender-blue flowers and attractive slender evergreen leaves.*

Cultivation

It will thrive in a hot sunny place in a poor, well-drained, and preferably limey soil. Plants may take some years to settle down and flower well, especially if they have become pot-bound before planting.

Propagation

The plants can be dug up in the autumn and pulled apart and the roots replanted. Well established, undisturbed groups usually seem to flower best.

Uses in the garden

Plant at the base of a sunny wall, perhaps amongst the roots of a shrub to give the hot, dry conditions required. Don't plant at the back of wide borders or the flowers will not be visible.

Alternatives

There is a number of named varieties available. 'Mary Barnard' is a good dark colour but later flowering and 'Walter Butt' is prolific, but rather pale.

CHOOSING PLANTS FOR SPECIAL PURPOSES

Plants for sunny sites
Abutilon × *suntense*
Ceanothus 'Autumnal Blue'
Convolvulus cneorum
Hebe 'Fairfieldii'
Yucca filamentosa

Plants for dry shade
Alchemilla mollis
Cotoneaster 'Cornubia'
Lunaria annua
Rubus tricolor
Vinca major 'Variegata'

Plants for damp shade
Camellia 'Donation'
Eleagnus pungens 'Maculata'
Hosta 'Frances Williams'
Impatiens 'Super Elfin'
Symphytum 'Hidcote Blue'

Plants for wet soil
Astilbe 'Sprite'
Lobelia 'Bees Flame'
Mimulus 'Malibu'
Salix caprea 'Pendula'
Sambucus racemosa 'Plumosa Aurea'

Plants for dry soil
Cheiranthus 'Bowles Mauve'
Euphorbia 'Lambrook Gold'
Lupinus varius
Melianthus major
Rosmarinus 'Miss Jessopp's Upright'

Plants for clay soil
Aster × *frikartii* 'Mönch'
Hamamelis mollis 'Pallida'
Helenium 'Coppelia'
Malus 'Golden Hornet'
Narcissus 'Geranium'

Plants for new gardens
Argyranthemum 'Jamaica Primrose'
Geranium endressii 'Wargrave Pink'
Laburnum × *watereri* 'Vossii'
Lamium maculatum 'Beacon Silver'
Ribes sanguineum 'Pulborough Scarlet'

Plants for shady walls
Chaenomeles 'Rowallane'
Hedera helix 'Glacier'
Hydrangea petiolaris
Pyracantha 'Mohave'
Tropaeolum peregrinum

Plants for sunny walls
Abutilon × *suntense*
Cytisus battandieri
Eccremocarpus scaber

Fremontodendron 'California Glory'
Solanum jasminoides 'Album'

Plants for acid soil
Epimedium alpinum
Gentiana sino-ornata
Lapageria rosea
Pieris 'Forest Flame'
Rhododendron 'Yellowhammer'

Plants for limy soil
Cheiranthus 'Blood Red'
Daphne mezereum
Dianthus 'Mrs Sinkins'
Helianthemum 'Wisley Pink'
Pulsatilla vulgaris

Tough plants
Alchemilla mollis
Bergenia 'Bressingham White'
Forsythia 'Lynwood'
Lonicera periclymenum 'Graham Thomas'
Symphytum 'Hidcote Blue'

Flowers for cutting
Crocosmia 'Lucifer'
Iris unguicularis
Lilium candidum
Ornithogalum nutans
Lathyrus 'Diamond Wedding'

Spring-flowering plants
Campanula cochlearifolia 'Cambridge Blue'
Narcissus 'February Gold'
Pieris 'Forest Flame'
Polyanthus 'Crescendo'
Pulmonaria saccharata 'Margery Fish'

Summer-flowering plants
Fremontodendron 'California Glory'
Lupinus arboreus
Nemesia 'Mello'
Rosa 'Zephirine Drouhin'
Salvia superba 'Lubecca'

Autumn-flowering plants
Acer palmatum 'Senkaki'
Anemone hybrida 'Honorine Joubert'
Clematis 'Bill McKenzie'
Cornus kousa var. *chinensis*
Gentiana sino-ornata

Winter-flowering plants
Erica herbacea 'Springwood White'
Forsythia 'Lynwood'
Helleborus orientalis
Sarcococca confusa
Viola 'Universal'

Long-flowering plants
Begonia 'Lucia'
Hypericum 'Hidcote'
Rosa 'Iceberg'
Solanum jasminoides 'Album'
Viola 'Maggie Mott'

Plants with attractive fruits
Daphne mezereum
Malus 'Golden Hornet'
Pyracantha 'Mohave'
Sarcococca confusa
Sorbus 'Joseph Rock'

Plants with good autumn colour
Acer griseum
Acer palmatum 'Dissectum Atropurpureum'
Cornus kousa var. *chinensis*
Euonymus alatus
Rhus typhina 'Laciniata'

Grey-leaved plants
Agropyron pubiflorum
Artimisia 'Powis Castle'
Convolvulus cneorum
Pyrus salicifolia 'Pendula'
Stachys lanata 'Silver Carpet'

Variegated plants
Hosta 'Shade Fanfare'
Mentha × *rotundifolia* 'Variegata'
Phalaris arundinacea 'Picta'
Salvia officinalis 'Icterina'
Weigela florida 'Variegata'

Yellow-leaved plants
Betula 'Golden Cloud'
Helichrysum petiolaris 'Limelight'
Robinia pseudacacia 'Frisia'
Sambucus racemosa 'Plumosa Aurea'
Thuja occidentalis 'Rheingold'

Plants for the back of border
Buddleia davidii 'Royal Red'
Chamaecyparis lawsoniana 'Lanei Aurea'
Laurus nobilis
Mahonia 'Charity'
Philadelphus 'Belle Etoile'

Plants for the middle of the border
Chrysanthemum 'Polar Star'
Crocosmia 'Lucifer'
Phalaris arundinacea 'Picta'
Phlox 'Border Gem'
Viburnum carlesii 'Aurora'

Plants for the front of border
Acaena 'Blue Haze'
Galanthus nivalis
Lavandula 'Hidcote'
Stachys lanata 'Silver Carpet'
Thymus × *citriodorus* 'Variegatus'

BUYING PLANTS AT THE GARDEN CENTRE

UNFORTUNATELY, NOT every plant on sale in garden centres is actually worth buying. My general impression is that the quality of the plants on sale is improving but even in some of the newer and widely promoted chains of centres, the plants can be very variable in quality.

So how can you make sure you get the best value when shopping for plants?

Trees

Generally sold in large pots, fruit trees are sometimes also sold with their roots wrapped in hessian or polythene.

Buy and plant in the autumn unless you are prepared to water diligently. Do not buy trees growing in what seems to be new compost and without at least some sign of roots around the drainage holes. And avoid plants marked 'do not lift this plant by its stem' as this means that they have only very recently been put in a larger pot and would pull out entirely if lifted by the stem.

Avoid plants with large quantities of stout roots emerging through the drainage holes, as they will have been in their pots for some time, could easily be starved and may not grow away well after planting.

Choose a tree with a straight stem and with its branches spaced evenly around it.

Check that the stem is not damaged or worn by overtight ties and that branches are not damaged or dead.

Buy a stake and a couple of tree ties for each tree.

Shrubs

Almost all shrubs are sold in pots although rhododendrons and conifers are sometimes sold with their roots wrapped in hessian.

Pot-grown plants can be planted at any time of year when the soil is not frozen or waterlogged; hessian-wrapped plants should be planted in the autumn.

Roses are sold for autumn planting with their roots wrapped in polythene and for spring-planting, they are grown in pots. Do not buy roses with polythene-wrapped roots in spring.

Do not buy shrubs that are wilting or dry, or are growing in what seems to be new compost and without at least a few roots growing through the drainage holes.

Choose plants without dead branches or shoots and with no apparent pests or diseases.

Plants with their branches spread in an even shape will make the most elegant specimens.

Avoid variegated plants that have plain green shoots.

Perennials

Perennials are almost always sold in pots. Avoid those with a large network of roots emerging through the drainage holes.

Do not buy perennials in summer as by that stage the pots are often too crammed with roots. Spring is the best time to buy.

Do not worry about a few dead leaves around the base of the plant but avoid plants with long lengths of bare and leafless stems.

Look for pots which are well filled, as these can sometimes be split into two or three fair-sized plants straight away.

Keep a watchful eye out for greenfly and other pests and diseases and avoid infected plants.

Bedding plants

Don't buy summer bedding plants until shortly before the likely last frost in your area, unless you have a greenhouse or conservatory to provide protection.

Pot-grown bedding plants will be larger than the plants in boxes and will establish themselves more quickly. They may also be better varieties but will probably be more expensive. Pot-grown plants are the best choice if you just want a few for tubs.

Plants in boxes or polystyrene strips will be smaller and cheaper, and may have become a little starved. These are more economical if you have a large area to plant.

Don't buy wilted or pest-infested plants or any with the shoot tips or leaf tips discoloured as they may have been frosted.

Plants without flowers usually establish better than those in flower. Many new varieties are bred specially to flower very early, even if their performance later in the season is less good.

Plants for spring flowering are usually on sale from early autumn and are available in pots, boxes or strips. They should be planted as soon as summer plants are over.

Wallflowers are usually dug from the open ground in the autumn and sold in kept in buckets of water. Look for plants which are fresh and not wilting. Avoid those with large amounts of soft and smelly lower foliage.

Bulbs

Spring-flowering bulbs are sold from late summer onwards. Buy them as soon as you are ready to plant them as they are better off in the ground rather than in the unsuitable conditions of the garden centre.

The fill-your-own-bag approach is often more economical than buying prepacked bulbs and enables you to reject soft or damaged bulbs.

Do not buy dry cyclamen, snowdrops or winter aconites as they are unlikely to grow well and have probably been dug up from the wild. Buy them 'in the green' (in growth) from specialist nurseries which have probably raised the plants themselves or buy them in pots at the garden centre.

BUYING PLANTS FROM SPECIALIST NURSERIES

Only a small number of the very best garden centres carry a good stock of the more unusual plants so if you want to buy anything a little out of the ordinary you'll often have to try specialist nurseries. Some of these operate on a mail-order-only basis and some are open only to callers; others deal with both callers and postal orders.

These specialist nurseries advertise in the gardening magazines and are also listed in *The Plant Finder* (see Recommended reading, page 154).

Most nurseries produce a catalogue or list which may vary from a photocopied, handwritten list to a colourful catalogue.

But those that are open to callers often have small quantities of other plants not included in the list. So a visit is always worthwhile.

Specialist nurseries rarely grow plants in huge quantities so it pays to send in your order or visit the nursery soon after the catalogue comes out otherwise they may have sold out of the varieties you want.

If you visit a specialist nursery, you will from a garden centre and you will almost always find staff who know their plants very well and can help you to choose the ones most suited to your needs.

BUYING PLANTS BY MAIL ORDER

MANY GARDENERS are sceptical of buying plants by mail order and it's true that you can't choose from the plants of any one variety that the nursery has in stock and the plants have a journey to contend with as well. But for many plants it's the only way.

So to take the worry out of buying by mail order, there are ways in which you can ensure that things go as smoothly as possible.
1 Find out how much the catalogue costs and send the right money.
2 Send off your order as soon as possible after you receive the catalogue.
3 Read the terms of business in the catalogue carefully and note in particular if you are required to send your money with the order and whether or not they suggest the use of a limit cheque.
4 Fill in the order form correctly, listing any substitutes if necessary. Don't forget your name and address!
5 Keep a copy of your order, preferably a

photocopy of the order form marked with the date you sent it off.
6 Check if the catalogue mentions when the plants are likely to be despatched and do not ring up or write about your order until that time is up.
7 Unpack your parcel carefully as soon as it arrives, checking that the plants are in good condition. If your soil is unsuitable for planting, store them somewhere cool and light.
8 If you have any cause for complaint or any problems with your order, always write to the nursery enclosing a copy of your order form.

Most nurseries offer a very dependable mail-order service. After all, their survival depends on the quality of their plants when the customer unpacks them. So don't hesitate to complain if you are dissatisfied.

But it can take quite a time to deal with telephone or written queries, so please try and be reasonable.

153

RECOMMENDED READING

General books

Three basic books from Reader's Digest will tell you most of the basics you need to know. Their *Encyclopaedia of Garden Plants and Flowers, Guide to Creative Gardening* and *The Garden Year* provide a mine of reliable information. The more recent *RHS Gardeners' Encyclopaedia of Plants and Flowers* is also amazingly comprehensive. For something more readable, you can't beat the books by Christopher Lloyd, especially *The Well-Tempered Garden* (Viking).

And then there's the indispensable *Plant Finder* (Headmain) which lists all the hardy and greenhouse plants available in the UK.

Trees and shrubs

Trees and shrubs are often grouped together in books and one of the best is *The Gardener's Illustrated Encyclopaedia of Trees and Shrubs* by Brian Davis (Viking). Hillier's *Manual of Trees and Shrubs* (David & Charles) is the most comprehensive volume giving short descriptions of almost all the trees and shrubs grown in the UK, including many rarities. The *Notcutts Book of Plants* (Notcutts) is especially useful in giving the size to which shrubs and trees grow over a tens year period.

Trees

Books specifically on trees are few but *Designing with Trees* by Yvonne Rees and Anthony Paul (Windward) gives good advice on how to use trees in the garden while *Gardening with Trees* by Sonia Kinahan (Christopher Helm) concentrates more on practical matters.

Shrubs

Most of the books dealing with both trees and shrubs are dominated by shrubs but on shrubs alone the beautifully illustrated *Shrubs* by Roger Phillips and Martin Rix (Pan) should be your first choice. For guidance on pruning you can do no better than *The Pruning of Trees, Shrubs and Conifers* by George Brown (Faber). On roses I suggest *Roses* by Roger Phillips and Martin Rix (Pan) and *Growing Roses* by Michael Gibson (Christopher Helm).

Finally, there are a number of small books in the Wisley Handbook series (RHS/Cassell) which are useful. These include *Camellias; Pruning Hardy Shrubs; Rhododendrons; Roses; Shrubs for Small Gardens.*

Climbers and wall shrubs

Your best buy is the most comprehensive book available, *Gardening on Walls* by Christopher Grey-Wilson and Victoria Mathews (Collins). Though it's a little short on cultivation and planting ideas, it's botanically accurate and includes all the climbers you are ever likely to meet. *Climbing Plants* by Kenneth A. Beckett (Christopher Helm) is also worth looking at and includes lists of climbers for different situations. *Climbers and Wall Plants* by George Preston (RHS/Cassell) is a good brief introduction.

For roses there's a good selection in *Roses* by Roger Phillips and Martin Rix (Pan) while *Climbing Roses Old and New* by Graham Stuart Thomas (Dent) is the most comprehensive book. On clematis go for *Clematis* by Christopher Lloyd and Tom Bennett or the more colourful but less entertaining *Clematis* by Barry Fretwell (Collins).

Perennials

Perennial Garden Plants by Graham Stuart Thomas (Dent) is a both erudite and readable reference book with some information on cultivation. The book entitled *Growing Hardy Perennials* by Kenneth A. Beckett (Christopher Helm) is actually more of an encyclopaedia.

Many books on specific plants are available including *Hellebores* by Brian Mathew (Alpine Garden Society), *Hardy Geraniums* by Peter Yeo, *Campanulas* by Peter Lewis and Margaret Lynch, *Ornamental Grasses* by Roger Grounds, *Meconopsis* by James Cobb (all Christopher Helm) and *Hostas* by Diana Grenfell (Batsford).

Foliage plants

The classic book on the subject is *Foliage Plants* by Christopher Lloyd (Viking) which is both informative and entertainingly written and there is also the more colourful *The Green Tapestry* by Beth Chatto (Collins). Both *Leaves* by Michael Jefferson-Brown (David and Charles) and *Foliage in Your Garden* by John Kelly (Windward) are more of introductions to the subject. Ursula Buchan's *Foliage Plants* (RHS/Cassell) is a briefer basic introduction.

Bulbs

There are quite a few good books on bulbs. Again Roger Phillips and Martin Rix have a colourful pictorial book, *Bulbs* (Pan), while for more of a reference book there is *The Smaller Bulbs* by Brian Mathew (Batsford); Brian Mathew's *The Year-Round Bulb Garden* (Souvenir Press) and his *Flowering Bulbs* (Collingridge) are both very accessible books on both the more familiar and more unusual garden bulbs. *Growing Dwarf Bulbs* by Jack Elliott (RHS/Cassell) is a good introduction to the subject.

There are a number of books on specific plants including *The Crocus* and also *The Iris* by Brian Mathew (Batsford), the slightly more practical *Iris* by Fritz Kohlein (Christopher Helm), *Lilies* by Victoria Mathews (Collingridge) and the more comprehensive *Growing Lilies* by Derek Fox (Christopher Helm).

Ground-cover plants

There are two outstanding books on ground-cover plants by two well-known writers. *Plants for Ground Cover* by Graham Stuart Thomas (Dent) is a comprehensive reference book which includes tabulated information on a huge range of plants. *Ground Cover Plants* by Margery Fish (Faber) is more chatty and is based on her experiences at East Lambrook Manor.

Shorter and more basic is *Ground Cover Plants* by Elspeth Napier and Fay Sharman (RHS/Cassell).

Annuals and bedding plants

There's only one comprehensive book on this subject, my own *Handbook of Annuals and Bedding Plants* (Christopher Helm). Mr Fothergill's Seeds publish a useful booklet called *Growing from Seed* and this gives a good introduction to the subject. Otherwise the seed catalogues probably provide the best sources of information.

Container plants

As usual there is a book in the Wisley Handbook series which provides an interesting introduction to the subject, *Gardening in Ornamental Containers* by Ray Waite (RHS/Cassell). An excellent and comprehensive book on the subject is *The Con-tained Garden* by Kenneth Beckett, David Carr and David Stevens (Windward).

Smaller plants

A Guide to Rock Gardening by Richard Bird is a very readable and practical introduction. This and *A Manual of Rock Garden Plants* edited by Chris Grey-Wilson are all part of a continuing series called the Rock Gardeners' Library (Christopher Helm). The *Manual of Alpine Plants* by Will Ingwersen (Collingridge) is the best reference book on the more unusual garden alpines.

A more colourful book but with less practical information is *Alpines for Your Garden* by Alan Bloom (Floraprint) while *Alpines* by Adrian Bloom (Jarrold) is a very short and colourful booklet. An *Illustrated Guide to Alpines* by Michael Upward, the secretary of the Alpine Garden Society, (Salamander), is one of the best books for real beginners.

Scented plants

As usual there is an excellent book in the Wisley Handbook series (RHS/Cassell); it's called *Fragrant and Aromatic Plants* by Kay Sanecki. She has also written a more comprehensive book called *The Fragrant Garden* (Batsford). *The Scented Garden* by Rosemary Verey (Michael Joseph) is just the book if scented plants interest you particularly. Older plants are featured in the fascinating *Plants from the Past* by David Stuart and James Sutherland (Viking) and there are also many scented plants discussed in *Cottage Garden Plants* by Roy Genders (Christopher Helm).

Herbs

Herb Gardening by Clare Lowenfield (Faber) will give enough information for newcomers to the subject and includes recipes. *Herbs in the Garden* by Allen Paterson (Dent) is more comprehensive.

Connoisseurs plants

Many of the books mentioned here include details of the more choice plants but two books which cover these in particular are *Success with Unusual Plants* by James Compton (Collins) and *Garden Plants for Connoisseurs* by Roy Lancaster (Unwin Hyman).

INDEX

Main entry page numbers are in bold and illustrations in italics

ACKNOWLEDGEMENTS

I would like to thank former *Practical Gardening* editor, Mike Wyatt, for agreeing to the suggestion that led to the first appearance of some of this material in the magazine as the 'Good Plants Guide' and for immediately recognizing how valuable it would be as a book.

Elaine Freeman's patient and cheerful help has been invaluable in keeping everything in order and especially in gathering together all the photographic material. I'd like to thank the current editor of the magazine, Adrienne Wild, for her support and her enthusiastic foreword.

Graham Rice
October 1989

PHOTOGRAPHIC CREDITS

Pat Brindley 65, 93, 131
Garden Picture Library 25, 28, 30, 40, 45, 62, 71(BL), 83, 85, 95, 101, 108, 109, 121, 124, 127(TR), 135, 137, 139, 148
Bob Gibbons (Natural Image) 49, 102, 114, 122, 123, 126/127
Iris Hardwick Picture Library 132
Mr Fothergill's Seeds 96
Practical Gardening 41
Graham Rice 39, 47, 64, 138
Chris Rose 20
Kenneth Scowen 53, 56, 115, 141, 144
Harry Smith 19, 34, 42, 66, 72, 73, 82, 84, 86, 89, 94, 104/5, 107, 111, 115, 119, 146/7
Michael Warren 9, 11, 12, 13, 14/15, 16, 17, 18, 21, 23, 24, 26, 27, 29, 31, 32, 33, 35, 36, 37, 38, 43, 44, 46, 48, 51, 54, 57(BR), 58, 59, 60, 61, 63, 67, 68, 69, 71(TL), 75, 76, 77, 78, 79, 80, 81, 87, 90, 91, 100, 103, 106, 110, 112, 117, 118, 125